AFTER TIPPECANOE

Some Aspects of the War of 1812

Edited by

PHILIP P. MASON

MICHIGAN STATE UNIVERSITY PRESS

EAST LANSING

♾ The paper used in this publication meets the minimum requirements of
ANSI/NISO Z39.48-1992 (R 1997) (Permanence of Paper).

Michigan State University Press
East Lansing, Michigan 48823-5245

Printed and bound in the United States of America.

17 16 15 14 13 12 11   1 2 3 4 5 6 7 8 9 10

LIBRARY OF CONGRESS CATALOGING-IN-PUBLICATION DATA

ISBN for this edition is 978-1-61186-002-3. The 1973 edition was catalogued by
the Library of Congress as follows:

Mason, Philip Parker, 1927–   ed.
   After Tippecanoe.
      p. cm.
   Includes bibliographical references.
   Reprint of the ed. published by Michigan State University Press,
   East Lansing.
   ISBN 0-8371-6903-8 (alk. paper)
1. United States –History –War of 1812 –Addresses, sermons, etc.   I. Utter,
William Thomas, 1895- II. Title.
[E364.5 .M3 1973]   973.5′2   73-7076

Cover design by Sharp Des!gns, Inc., Lansing, MI
Book design by Aptara, Inc.
Cover art is "Battle of Thames—Death of Tecumseh" originally published in
Spencer, J. A., *History of the United States, 3 volumes* (New York, NY: Johnson, Fry,
and Company, 1858).

g green   Michigan State University Press is a member of the Green Press
   press   Initiative and is committed to developing and encouraging
ecologically responsible publishing practices. For more information about the
Green Press Initiative and the use of recycled paper in book publishing, please
visit www.greenpressinitiative.org.

Visit Michigan State University Press on the World Wide Web at:
www.msupress.msu.edu

After Tippecanoe

Some Aspects of the War of 1812

CONTENTS

FOREWORD
A NOTE ON THE ORIGIN OF THIS BOOK

Hazen E. Kunz

After Tippecanoe: Some Aspects of the War of 1812 consists of six lectures presented in 1961-62 in Detroit and Windsor, Canada. Known as the Quaife-Bayliss Lectures, they were sponsored by the Algonquin Club, an international organization of men interested in the history of the border region between Michigan and Ontario.

One of the Club's founders in 1934 was Dr. Milo M. Quaife, one of the foremost authorities on the history of the Old Northwest. For thirteen years, Dr. Quaife presided over the Algonquin Club; after that, as honorary life president, he continued to be a faithful and inspiring member. It was during this long association with the Club that he became so intimately acquainted with Mr. Joseph E. Bayliss who, although residing at Sault Ste. Marie, was an enthusiastic Algonquin member. It was through their mutual interest in Great Lakes and regional history that Dr. Quaife and Mr. Bayliss established their firm friendship.

On September 1, 1959, while on his way to Sault Ste. Marie to visit his long-time friend and literary collaborator, Dr. Milo M. Quaife was fatally injured in an automobile accident. Soon after this Mr. Bayliss also died, leaving to the Algonquin Club a generous bequest to be used as the membership saw fit for the advancement of interest in local history.

The sesquicentennial of the War of 1812 with its regional implications suggested itself as a proper subject for the Algonquin Club. The Club decided in 1960 to devote a portion of the Bayliss bequest to sponsoring a series of six lectures, by eminent American and Canadian scholars, on the War of 1812, with particular emphasis on events in the Michigan-Ontario region.

A Committee was appointed consisting of Frank B. Woodford, Philip P. Mason, Alan R. Douglas, Archie Brighton, Robert E. Lee, and Ronald

McKee. This Committee began work immediately and invited six distinguished authorities, three from the United States, and three from Canada, to give a series of talks during the 1961-62 season. The programs, which alternated between Detroit and Windsor, attracted over a thousand persons.

The lectures were presented as a memorial to Dr. Quaife and Mr. Bayliss, in the hope that commemoration of events of one hundred and fifty years ago that helped shape the future of Michigan and Ontario will further cement the bonds of friendship and mutual interest that join the people of the United States and of Canada.

PREFACE

Philip P. Mason

As Hazen E. Kunz, then president of the Algonquin Club, pointed out in the foreword to *After Tippecanoe: Some Aspects of the War of 1812,* the lectures published here were presented in Windsor, Ontario, and Detroit, Michigan, during the winter of 1961–62.

In addition to the six main speakers, all of them distinguished authorities in their respective research and writings on the War of 1812, the Algonquin Club also invited Dr. Fred Coyne Hamil, professor of history at Wayne State University, to prepare an overview of the war, especially as it affected Michigan and Ontario. Hamil was educated at Queens College in Kingston, Ontario, at Columbia University, and at the University of Michigan, which in 1933 awarded him a PhD in history. He was author of *The Valley of the Lower Thames, 1640 to 1850,* and *Lake Erie Baron: The Story of Colonel Thomas Talbot.*

In Hamil's introduction, he points out that the year 1811 marked the culmination of the Indians' efforts to resist the American penetration of their lands in the Old Northwest. By that point the Shawnee chief Tecumseh and his brother Tenskwatawa, known as "The Prophet," had been engaged for nearly two years in an attempt to form a confederacy of tribes to preserve the old ways of life and stem the tide of white settlement. However, in November 1811, following Tecumseh's refusal to recognize a new cession of lands along the Wabash River, the Americans marched to the edge of his village, Prophetstown, at the mouth of Tippecanoe Creek. This triggered the Indians to launch an attack that was doomed to failure and an end to all hope of an Indian federation.

The Battle of Tippecanoe also gave fuel to the war party in Congress, which blamed the British for providing arms to the Indians and clamored ever more loudly for war to end England's power in North America. Thus, it may be claimed that Tippecanoe was the overture to the War of 1812.

The war was a strange one, and, to paraphrase a statement made by Woodrow Wilson while he was a young professor at Princeton University, the results of the war were "singularly uncertain." However, the fact remains that in the two centuries since then Canada and America have shared a continent in peaceful and friendly cooperation.

The first presenter at the Quaife-Bayliss Lectures, Dr. William T. Utter, professor of history at Denison University, received his education at Northwest Missouri Teachers College and the University of Chicago, which awarded him a PhD in history in 1929. He taught history at Ohio State University from 1924 to 1929 before joining the faculty at Denison. He was the author of *Granville: The Story of an Ohio Village* and *The Frontier State, 1803–1825*.

Dr. Utter died shortly after his lecture, but fortunately a tape recording of his talk was preserved, and from it a transcript was prepared for this book. As editor of the collection, I made minor changes to the transcript and added citations to quotations. Although Professor Utter intended to delete his extemporaneous remarks at the beginning and ending of his lecture, I believe they bear repeating to illustrate his personal interest in the War of 1812. He opened his lecture as follows:

> When I attended Charter Oak, a rural grammar school near Los Angeles, we learned to sing all the verses of *The Star Spangled Banner,* including the verse which started with the question: *And where is that band who so vauntingly swore / That the havoc of war and the battle's confusion / A home and a country should leave us no more?* The poet's answer to his own question was this: *Their blood has wash'd out their foul footstep's pollution.* Even to a ten-year-old this answer seemed a bit sanguinary, and I had trouble picturing just what was going on. We learned that the central idea in the national anthem was in the lines: *Then conquer we must, when our cause it is just. And this be our motto—In God is our Trust.* Miss Thompson taught us about the War of 1812 in the spirit of those words. I could take a lot of time discussing the modifications which have come to my understanding of that war in the years since.

The epilogue to Dr. Utter's speech helps explain the warm rapport he established with his audience.

> I am sure that I have never before deliberately added an epilogue to a speech, although on occasion I have had to defend myself. I ask your indulgence in this matter because I had a stake in the campaign around Detroit; and so did Granville, the village where I live. My father's two grandfathers, Robert Utter and Samuel Rogers, were up here. Robert was fairly safe, for he was with Hull; Samuel Rogers was in greater danger, for he narrowly escaped death at Fort Meigs. My

personal concern lies in the fact that my grandparents had not yet been born. Suppose Samuel had been killed by one of the bullets that hit him—where would I be? If you have an answer, I should like to have it, although I suppose there is no urgency about it.

The village of Granville, founded in 1805, had a band made up of the following instruments: two clarinets, two oboes, two bassoons, and a bass drum. They had been playing for five years or so before the coming of the war and enlisted as a unit. They marched with Hull from Urbana, Ohio, to the Maumee. Their position in the line of march was immediately behind the General, the safest place they could have found, everything considered. Hull reached the lake without knowing that war had been declared and put some important supplies, papers, etc., on a schooner, which the Canadians captured. I regret to say that the band instruments were included. It seems clear that the musicians got their instruments back after the surrender, for this bassoon is known to have been among them. I shall try to make some intelligible noises for you. But please remember that the combined age of the bassoon and the bassoonist amounts to more than two hundred years. The first tune doesn't count; I am really making sure that the thing will play.

A contemporary account of Hull's surrender states that a band played *God Save the King*. If I were only a novelist I could make up a good story based on this simple fact, and for the moment let me pretend that I am. The humiliated American soldiers walked slowly past the table where they were signing their paroles. Among the first were the boys of the Granville band. The British officer, recognizing them, asked, "I suppose you men want your instruments back, don't you?" They assured him that they did. "Very well, then, you may have them if you play *God Save the King*."

Professor Utter ended his speech with a rendition of *God Save the King* on the original bassoon from the Granville band.

Dr. W. Kaye Lamb, Dominion Archivist and National Librarian, Dominion of Canada, lectured on "Sir Isaac Brock: The Hero of Queenston Heights." In his paper, which was based upon extensive research on one of Canada's great leaders and utilizing the large holdings of Brock's personal and official papers in Canada and the United Kingdom, Dr. Lamb described how Major General Brock intercepted the outbreak of hostilities with the United States and prepared defenses along the Canadian and American borders. Under his leadership he forced General Hull to surrender Detroit and thereby greatly improved the morale of Canadian militia, the people of Canada, and their Indian allies. In October 1811 General Brock, anticipating an American attack on Fort George on the Niagara Peninsula, rallied his troops, defeated the invaders, and won the titles "Hero of Queenston Heights" and "Savior of Canada."

Dr. Lamb was educated at the University of British Columbia, from which he received BA and MA degrees and in 1933 a PhD from the London School of Economics. In 1948 Dr. Lamb became the fourth Dominion Archivist of Canada and the country's first National Librarian, positions he held until his retirement in 1969. Not only did he establish a modern archival system in Canada, but he also continued his historical research. Among his many publications were *The Hero of Upper Canada; The History of Canada from Discovery to Present Day; Sixteen Years in the Indian Country: The Journal of Daniel Williams Harmon;* and *Letters and Journals of Simon Fraser.*

Dr. G. F. Stanley was educated at the University of Alberta and Oxford University. He went on to become chairman of the Faculty of Arts and head of the Department of History, Royal Military College, Kingston, Ontario. In his lecture, Stanley discussed the relative importance of the roles played by the Canadian militia and the British regular troops in "The Contribution of the Canadian Militia during the War." His detailed account of the various militia campaigns on the Canadian-American border was based on extensive research and major publications, including *Birth of Western Canada: The Story of the Riel Rebellion, Canada's Soldiers in the Face of Danger, The History of the Lake Superior Regiment,* and *For Want of a Horse: A Journal of General Burgoyne's Expedition, 1777.*

Colonel C. P. Stacey, professor of history, University of Toronto, in his insightful lecture, "Naval Power on the Lakes, 1812–1814," argued that naval power was the determining influence in military operations in the Great Lakes Basin and the deciding factor of the major battles of the war. The defense of the Michigan-Ontario frontier was based upon communications, he explained. In "the best-settled parts of Canada, roads were vile," and "only by water could men or goods be moved with ease and speed." However, Colonel Stacey argued, American lines of communication between the East Coast and the upper Great Lakes were better, especially between New York, Philadelphia, and Lake Ontario and Lake Erie. Thus, the United States was able to establish naval yards at Sackets Harbor on Lake Ontario and at Erie, Pennsylvania, where a fleet of warships was built. Under the command of Captain Oliver Hazard Perry, the Americans won a bitter and decisive naval battle over the British at Put-in-Bay, Lake Erie, in September 1813. Colonel Stacey did not describe the Battle of Lake Erie, and although he concluded that "it was more a logical than a tactical victory," he recognized it as one of the most decisive battles of the war.

Dr. Reginald Horsman, professor of history at the University of Wisconsin–Milwaukee, discussed "The Role of the Indian in the War" in his lecture. Based upon his book *The Causes of the War of 1812,* Dr. Horsman explained the various reasons for the Indians' allegiance to Britain and the significant part they played in British defense of Ontario. Of particular interest to Algonquin Club members was the role of the Shawnee, Wyandot, Delaware, Miami, Ottawa, Chippewa, and Pottawatomie tribes under British Indian agent Matthew Elliot in the Amherstburg-Detroit border region. The background of the surrender of Detroit by General William Hull, its impact upon the morale of American soldiers, and the defeat of the British and their Indian allies under Tecumseh are covered in detail.

Dr. Thomas D. Clark added an important chapter on the War of 1812 in his carefully researched and annotated paper "Kentucky in the Northwest Campaign." He described in detail how Senator Henry Clay opened his famous "War Hawk Campaign" in 1811 over the issues of British Impressment, Orders in Council, and the Napoleonic decrees. Clay and his colleagues even maintained that the Kentucky militia could on its own carry out the conquest of Canada. Kentucky volunteers fought in the Battle of Tippecanoe under General William Henry Harrison, and after the war was officially declared, two thousand Kentuckians joined the militia to fight the British and their Indian allies. Several hundred of them arrived in southern Michigan in the winter of 1812–13 to join Governor William Hull and the invasion of Canada. After a bitter battle on the River Raisin at Frenchtown (now Monroe, Michigan) in January 1813, following Hull's surrender of Detroit the Kentucky militia officers also surrendered with the assurance by British officers that the wounded Kentucky militiamen would be protected from Indian excesses. This promise was not kept, and when the British soldiers left, the Indians murdered and scalped the wounded. Kentucky residents were enraged and bitter about this massacre, and throughout the rest of the war, "Remember the Raisin" was the battle cry of Kentuckians.

Dr. Clark, chairman of the Department of History at the University of Kentucky, began his education at the Universities of Mississippi, Virginia, and Kentucky. He was awarded a PhD from Duke University in 1932. Among his many publications were *Pills, Petticoats and Plows, Frontier America,* and *The Great American Frontier.*

After Tippecanoe

INTRODUCTION

Fred Coyne Hamil

THE TREATY that ended the War of American Independence in 1783 failed to provide a foundation for a firm and lasting peace between England and her former colonies. British fur traders protested the surrender of the territory south of the Great Lakes, and the Indian allies of the British felt themselves betrayed by the failure to protect their ancestral hunting grounds. Regretting the decision made at the treaty table, and hoping still to retain the West, the British made no move to carry out their agreement to relinquish, with all convenient speed, the posts at Michilimackinac, Detroit, Niagara, and elsewhere. The excuse given was the alleged failure of the United States to fulfill the terms of the treaty concerning the property rights of the Loyalists, and of the British merchants.

The forces of disintegration in the United States, which the British hoped would cause its collapse, were soon checked by the new federal constitution. American irritation grew as the British continued to retain the western posts and to occupy American soil. The British were also blamed for inciting the Indians to make war against the Americans, and for providing them with arms. Although the British really desired peace, they did not wish to incur the hostility of the Indians by abandoning them completely. But in 1794 the dream of an Indian buffer state in the Ohio region was ended by the victory of General Anthony Wayne over the Indians at Fallen Timbers, on the lower Maumee River; and in the following year, at Greenville, the Indians were forced to cede to Congress most of their remaining lands in Ohio. These events, and the mission of John Jay to London, induced Great Britain to agree to evacuate the western posts in 1796.

The British did not consent, however, to give up the right of search of American ships, which had already caused ill-feeling between the two countries during the course of England's war with France. In the years that followed, the British frequently aroused American anger both by searching American ships and by impressing sailors, some of whom claimed American citizenship. In 1807 war was barely averted when the British ship *Leopard* attacked the American warship *Chesapeake;* incidents arose as the English asserted, and exercised, the right to seize neutral ships carrying contraband to the enemy. Napoleon's attempt, by his Continental System, to exclude British goods from Europe, was countered by the Orders-in-Council, which forced neutral ships to go first to Britain before entering a European port. Jefferson's retaliatory embargo in 1807, and the later Nonintercourse Acts, were ineffective, except to harm American trade.

Meanwhile, the troubles in the West were not ended by Jay's Treaty and the resulting relinquishment of the western posts by the British. Many Indian tribes came to Amherstburg and other Canadian posts to trade, and to secure arms and supplies which they carried back to their villages in American territory. The Canadian authorities, fearing the outbreak of war between England and the United States, made special efforts to secure the attachment of the Indians by generous gifts, thus confirming the Americans in their belief that the British were plotting a renewal of the Indian war. The efforts of the Canadians to strengthen their defenses were regarded in the United States as further evidence of their hostile intentions.

The year 1811 marked the culmination of the Indians' efforts to resist the pressure of American encroachment on their lands. For nearly two years the Shawnee chief Tecumseh and his brother the Prophet had been engaged in an attempt to form a confederacy of the tribes, for the purpose of preserving the old ways of life and stemming the tide of white settlement. In November 1811, following Tecumseh's refusal to recognize a new cession of lands along the Wabash River, Governor William Henry Harrison of the Indiana Territory collected a large army and advanced up the Wabash to the Prophet's village at the mouth of Tippecanoe Creek. In Tecumseh's absence the Indians attacked the American camp, and after a fierce battle were decisively beaten. The movement for an Indian federation was ended. As before, the British were blamed for providing the Indians with arms, and for inciting them to attack. In the new Congress the War Hawks from the western states, and from the frontier districts of others, now clamored loudly for war to end England's power in North America. In May 1811 popular feeling was inflamed by the naval conflict between the *President* and the *Little Belt.* As a result of Napoleon's pretense in 1810 of ending his commercial restrictions, American resentment was now concentrated against Britain. The latter refused to abandon impressment, and her repeal of the hated Orders-in-Council came too late. On June 18, 1812, Congress declared war against her.

The causes of the war have been termed "uncertain," but perhaps "complex" is the proper word, as the late Dr. William Utter illustrated in his paper, "The Coming of the War of 1812." As usual there was "multiple causation," with impressment of American seamen, British Orders-in-Council, western land hunger, the Indian menace, and national pride all playing a part; but which of these was primary and which were secondary? Utter tended to support the view, taken originally by President James Madison in his War Message, that impressment was the deciding factor, but he was careful to emphasize that due weight must be given to all the others. This view is gaining ground again today, but scholars have not yet been able to reach a consensus on the relative importance of American maritime grievances and the problems in the West.

Not only the causes but the very nature of the conflict appear in altered perspective from the viewpoint of an Englishman, a Canadian, or an American. The people of Britain, engaged in a long and desperate struggle with the Napoleonic Empire, could not but see the war with the United States as a troublesome, but unavoidable and relatively unimportant, side issue. Their government had preferred to risk war with the militarily weak country on the other side of the Atlantic, as long as advantage ensued from policies so obnoxious to the United States. When war came Britain relied on the Canadian militia and a small force of regular soldiers, assisted by the British navy, to contain the advance of the numerically powerful American armies against Canada. Only after Napoleon had been defeated in 1814 were any numbers of British troops sent out to North America. Englishmen still tend to view the War of 1812 in the broader perspective of the world conflict in which they were then engaged.

Loyal Canadians, especially in the years following the war, saw the American attack upon their country as naked, unprovoked aggression, an attempt by a powerful and greedy neighbor to conquer their land and subject them to a hated republican rule. Nor was this conviction affected by the thought that, as long as Britain controlled the seas, the United States could not really come to grips with her great enemy except through the British North American provinces; and that the hostile Indians looked to Canada for support. These Canadians found confirmation for their beliefs in the fiery speeches of the War Hawks in and out of Congress, and in many of the American newspapers. The patriotism that arose among Canadians during the war was fanned later by what Dr. G. F. G. Stanley has described as "the national myth of the loyal militiaman springing to arms in 1812 and saving the country from its forcible incorporation in the United

States," a country so overwhelmingly superior in men and resources. This incipient Canadian nationalism was long associated with a bitter hatred of Americans and everything that could be considered American, although in some sections, particularly in western Upper Canada (now Ontario), large numbers of the inhabitants were American-born and naturally did not share this feeling. And as additional American settlers, accustomed to democratic institutions and ideas, continued to cross the border after the war, the resulting dichotomy of sentiment in Upper Canada, deepened by the spread of radicalism from the British Isles, became a major factor in the abortive rebellion of 1837.

Stanley, in "The Contribution of the Canadian Militia During the War," discusses the relative importance of the part played in the war by the Canadian militia and the British regular troops. Because the militia was involved in every action on the Canadian-American border, including numerous minor incidents, as well as guard duty, Stanley's paper includes a detailed account of the various campaigns there. Dr. W. Kaye Lamb, in "Sir Isaac Brock: the Hero of Queenston Heights," covers a portion of the same ground, but is chiefly concerned with characterizing Brock and explaining the part played by this brilliant military leader in Upper Canada before and after the beginning of the war, until he met an heroic death on the Niagara frontier. Colonel C. P. Stacey, in "Naval Power on the Lakes, 1812-1814," reaffirms Admiral Mahan's classic exposition of the influence of sea power, particularly on the Great Lakes, during the course of the War of 1812. Here lies, in part, the explanation of Hull's surrender at Detroit, Procter's abandonment of Fort Malden and defeat on the Thames, and other events of the war, although the personal qualities of the leaders must not be neglected. In the last analysis the United States failed to conquer Canada because of her deficiencies in planning, strategy and generalship. A successful attack on Montreal would have caused all of Canada west of that point to fall like ripe fruit, although British sea power might very well have retained Quebec and the Maritime Provinces.

The three chapters mentioned above are confined to the course of the war on the Canadian-American border. Dr. Reginald Horsman, in "The Role of the Indian in the War," describes the position of the Indians, their long struggle to preserve their lands and way of life in the face of American settlement, and their considerable contribution to the British cause in the war, especially in the West. Dr. Thomas D. Clark, in "Kentucky in the Northwest Campaign," recounts the activities of the soldiers, and the people generally, of one of the American states that engaged most wholeheartedly in the war. In the region dealt with by these papers most of the land "battles" were mere skirmishes in the wilderness or areas of sparse settlement, involving no more than a few hundred men on either side. They conformed generally to the pattern of the centuries-old border warfare between French and Indians and English colonists, which had continued through the American Revolutionary War. One of the bloodiest and most decisive conflicts was on water: the Battle of Lake Erie. But for Canadians and Americans the War of 1812 has a significance that is not measured by the size of its battles or the numbers of its dead.

Canada suffered greatly from the war, as did parts of the United States, in the destruction of property and in the blood and treasure expended. At the Peace Canada was forced to relinquish forever the hope of regaining that part of the old Empire of the St. Lawrence, with its fur trade, which lay to the south of the Great Lakes. The Treaty of Ghent also dealt a mortal blow to the cause of the Indians, who claimed domanial rights to the hunting grounds of their ancestors in the region of the Ohio and the Mississippi. No longer could they hope to stem the tide of settlement and preserve their ancient way of life. The tenuous unity of action among them that Tecumseh's leadership had produced ended with his death in the Battle of the Thames on October 5, 1813. This was the end also of the British support of the Indians in their resistance to the westward movement of the Americans.

The issues were not so clear to the people of the United States as they were to their enemies. Sectional differences gave rise to a variety of responses, ranging from luke-warm support or outright opposition in New England (as also in some parts of the British-American provinces), to the frenzied war fever in Kentucky which is described by Utter and Clark. Although Utter suggested a caveat, it appears that in many parts of the United States, as in Canada, a fresh wave of patriotism and national pride was engendered by the war. Clark shows how it enhanced the reputations and made heroes of some of the officers from Kentucky, who later used their fame for political advancement. But if the will-of-the-wisp of military ambition proved a friendly spirit to Johnson, Harrison and Shelby, it lured others to destruction.

The War of 1812 has been termed, as far as the United States was concerned, a war that more than usually was unnecessary and futile. The treaty that brought it to a close provided for the restoration of the territorial *status quo ante bellum,* and it seemed that the United States had failed to achieve any of the objects for which she had gone to war. But in the lengthening perspective of time the magnitude of the war's effect upon her, as upon Canada, has become increasingly clear. Many Americans came to regard it as a "second war of independence" from British oppression; some had welcomed it from the beginning, as the only way to compel proud England to respect the rights of the United States as a free nation. There is some truth in these views.

The Treaty of Ghent provided for the establishment of joint commissions to adjudicate outstanding disputes between the two countries over boundaries and fisheries. Occasional crises arose, however, both over these questions and over attacks on Canada by "Patriots" and Fenians from the United States, as well as over various incidents that occurred during the American Civil War. England's determination to avoid another war with the United States, even at the sacrifice of cherished Canadian interests, was no small factor in the keeping of the peace and the ultimate settlement of these problems. In 1817 the Rush-Bagot Agreement, concluded for reasons of economy and as a result of lessons learned during the war, provided for the virtual elimination of naval armaments on the Lakes. Although the Agreement was not concerned with border fortifications, it was the first step towards what in the process of time came to be truly the "unguarded frontier," and the present era of friendship and cooperation between the two nations.

THE COMING OF THE WAR

William T. Utter

THROUGHOUT the nineteenth century, historians interpreted the causes of the War of 1812 with remarkable consistency. They simply enlarged upon President Madison's War Message. Henry Adams, in his magnificent history of the period, had thrown some doubts on Madison's reasons for the declaration.[1] But it was not until the early decades of this century that younger and more critical historians began to wrestle with the problem of the causes of the war. In 1902 Woodrow Wilson, a young professor at Princeton University, wrote a pot-boiler which he called *A History of the American People*.[2] At the conclusion of his discussion of the outbreak of the war, he wrote this sentence: "The grounds of the war were singularly uncertain." Let me give you my assurance that historians dislike writing a sentence like that and that you can take Professor Wilson's phrase literally.

In the first quarter of this century the influence of Frederick Jackson Turner became dominant among scholars who were studying early American history. Turner's name is forever associated with the history of the American frontier, but his true interest seems to have been in the analysis of sectionalism, with emphasis on the West. The sectional nature of the support of the war had long been noted; as it was now studied in detail, a sort of double paradox became apparent. The declaration of war had received its greatest support from the West and the South, whereas the maritime sections, notably New England, were strong in their opposition—and this in spite of the fact that the war was being fought ostensibly for maritime rights. This paradox could be approached in many ways, no doubt, but the first, and possibly the most plausible, critic of the older interpretation was Louis M. Hacker, then a young professor at Columbia University, who in 1924 contributed an essay to the *Mississippi Valley Historical Review* entitled "Western Land Hunger and the War of 1812: A Conjecture."[3] The word "conjecture" might seem to indicate an uncertainty on the part of the writer, an uncertainty which does not appear in the essay

9

itself. Hacker abandoned almost completely Madison's list of causes for the war, on the ground that he saw no association between those causes and the enthusiasm which westerners were displaying for the war. The true key to the paradox of the western attitude lay in covetousness, Mr. Hacker said. We were sinning; we coveted our neighbors' lands. He asserted that Canada represented the greatest reserves of agricultural lands immediately accessible to westerners. To make his thesis more tenable, Hacker minimized even the Indian danger and exaggerated the hesitation which frontiersmen felt toward settling in the prairies—perhaps based on the assumption that prairies which could not grow trees could not grow crops.

Mr. Hacker's point of view was much criticized, and answered in part, but never completely refuted. My own reaction is that he did not search very ardently for contemporary evidence which might not support his theory. For example, he lists at some length toasts drunk at various banquets which made allusion to the glories of a war in which Canada would be conquered. These toasts were taken largely from a Zanesville paper. I could match this evidence, toast for toast, with expressions of the contrary point of view from such towns as Putnam and Marietta, where Federalist sympathies were much in evidence.

It is a little as if historians had turned psychiatrists, got Madison and his lieutenants on the leather couch, and addressed them: "We know that the reasons you give for this declaration are not the true reasons. Now give us the truth, preferably something sinful."

We must distinguish between two ways of putting the matter. Historian A will say: there were a number of reasons why we were justified in declaring war against Britain. If we were to fight Great Britain we could do so only in Canada. In this way the conquest of Canada became, of necessity, one of our war aims. Historian B will say: we wanted Canada and therefore pretended that we were fighting Britain for causes one, two, three (the maritime causes), while it was understood among ourselves that our real reason was to conquer Canada. For historian B, expansionism becomes the primary cause. With all deference to Mr. Hacker, I feel that he used the latter approach.

In 1925 there appeared a volume entitled *Expansionists of 1812,* by Julius W. Pratt.[4] I remember when the book appeared, because Dr. Pratt was ending his graduate study at the University of Chicago at the time I was in the midst of mine. I regarded him then and do now as an exceptionally able scholar. The title of the book has a ring to it; for the first time a thorough study was made, fully documented, of sectional contentions over the declaration of war. Dr. Pratt not only looked into the western desire for Canadian land and the whole problem of the Indians, but really broke new ground in his study of southern ambitions for Spanish territory along the Gulf. This book has had enormous influence, particularly among writers of text-books in American history. As a result, recent students of American history have been rather thoroughly indoctrinated in the "land hunger" theory, and are ready to make statements far more critical than those of Dr. Pratt. He is a judicious scholar, and at the close of the introduction to his work he wrote, in regard to the scope and pro-portions of his study, that it makes no effort to give a *full* account of the causes of the War of 1812 but deals with one set of causes only. He goes on to say that despite his failure to deal with the maritime grievances he was convinced that without them there would have been no war. He felt that it was also safe to say, however, that without the peculiar grievances and ambitions of the West there would have been no war. One set of causes was in his mind as essential as the other. It is no fault of Dr. Pratt that textbook writers as well as col-lege students have failed to read what he wrote in his introduction. Whatever Dr. Pratt may have wished, his book fastened the "land hunger" theory firmly in the minds of students of American history. Dr. Pratt's is the best study of rival factions and personalities in this period of acute political fractiousness. He shows that Secretary of State James Monroe hardly mentioned the notion that the conquest of Canada was a war aim. He shows, too, the contentions between the northern and southern wings of the Republican party, each with hopes for territorial aggrandizement. Once again I raise my earlier questions: are the conquests of Canada and the Gulf Coast to be considered as primary or secondary factors in the declaration of war? If you hold that they were primary, then you place a charge of hypocrisy against Americans in high places.

A valid criticism of the "land hunger" thesis is that it is too sim-ple an explanation of a complex matter. If I were asked what school of historiography I belong to I should probably reply that I am of the school of multiple causation, which is no school at all. Woodrow Wilson found that the grounds for the war were singularly uncertain; here, if anywhere in American history, one must list all the factors which entered into the decision made in Washington and give the various factors their appropriate weight, thus avoiding the absurdity of explaining everything by a single motive. Land hunger and the In-dian menace would doubtless be given considerable weight; so, too, would the genuine grievances which we had against Britain.

Let me list a few factors to which I would give attention, but possibly not a great deal of weight. I have always been intrigued by the fact that almost within the week in which we declared war, Napoleon set in motion his invasion of Russia. Would we have declared war if we could have foreseen the disaster which was about to overwhelm the great French leader? This is almost the equivalent of saying, although we did not admit it even to ourselves, that we were betting on Napoleon's continued success, that we were tying our future to his. This is not the equivalent of saying that we approved of what he was doing, as the Federalists generally charged. Readers of the four-page weekly papers of the frontier towns were able to follow the career of Napoleon in great detail. The news was not generally colored in his favor.

American resentment at restrictions on our commerce might have been directed as well at Napoleon as at the British, and some hot-headed patriots wanted us to commit the absurdity of declaring war against both. In our exasperation against both parties, we chose to fight the one which was the more accessible.

Then there is the less tangible matter of a war to defend national honor. I have never forgotten that the Ladies Aid Society of one of the Chillicothe churches passed resolutions which were most belligerent, at the time of the *Chesapeake-Leopard* episode. Let me read you a brief extract from a letter written by a friend to Senator Worthington.[5] The date was late December, 1811: ". . . in the event of an army of the United States being sent to affect the conquest of Cannady we wont have no invation to apprehend from the British on that quarter, indeed from every view I can take of the subject I have been unable to discover on what quarter the British could do the U. S. any material injury and we would invade and conquer Cannady and humble their overbearing pride." Dr. Pratt quotes this letter to uphold the "land hunger" idea.[6] It might be quoted with equal weight to uphold the idea that there was general resentment of England's air of condescension towards us, even her hesitancy in apologizing for her flagrant abuse of power in the *Chesapeake-Leopard* affair. It is certainly difficult to evaluate a factor such as this, but that it was a factor few could doubt.

Here is a short passage written by a young patriot shortly after Hull's surrender.[7] His letter speaks of "the most shameful surrender that ever took place in the world. Our brave captain Harry James cursed and swore like a pirate, and cried like his heart would break. He's got the true blood of his uncle John James flowing in his veins. He would fight a regiment of British. He has treasured up all the stories of the suffering of his forefathers in South Carolina during the war of liberty in '76 and he hates the damned rascals as bad as I do. Give my love to my father and tell him I have suffered greater hardships in six months than he did in North Carolina during the war for liberty."

Many other letters in this vein could be found. One might be tempted to conclude that the younger generation, becoming bored with their fathers' stories of their heroism in the war for liberty, decided to go out and fight the British so that they would have some stories of their own. Or one might choose simply to say the participants in this war fought for the love of their country. But I must not continue in this line for fear you charge me with being facetious.

Another argument, both new and old, regards the matter of impressment as the leading cause of the conflict. President Madison said it was, and if I should attempt for a short time to uphold this position it would in a sense be to come full circle, back to the point of origin.

In October 1811, some eight months before the declaration of war, J. Q. Adams wrote to Secretary of War William Eustis, "The practice of impressment is the only inerradicable wound, which if persisted in can terminate no otherwise than by war. But it seems clearly better to wait our increasing strength and our adversary's more mature decay before we undertake to abolish it by war."[8] This was the summary of a very wise and widely experienced American, a man of a good deal of objectivity. He went on to say that he did not think that the nation should declare war explicitly on the point of impressment. Dr. James F. Zimmerman, who wrote a dissertation at Columbia University on the matter of impressment, holds that Madison was in substantial agreement with Adams' point of view.[9] Madison, in other words, was willing to postpone a declaration. The leadership of the new Congress made this difficult if not impossible. This view would certainly be that held by Senator Thomas Worthington, one of the great leaders in Ohio, who felt so keenly that our nation was unprepared for war that he voted against the declaration, although he would have conceded that we had causes which would have justified us.

In his war message of June 1, the President placed impressment first in his list of British aggressions. "Thousands of American citizens under the safeguard of public law and of the national flag have been torn from their country and everything dear to them, have been exposed under the severity of their disciplines to be exiled to the most distant and deadly climes, risk their lives in the battles of their oppressors and to be the melancholy instruments of taking away those of their own brethren. Against this crying enormity, which Great Britain would be so prompt to avenge if committed against herself, the United States have in vain exhausted remonstrances and expostulations. . . ."[10] Those who voted against the declaration generally agreed that impressment was an almost intolerable grievance but that it should be the subject of further negotiations. Congress had already indicated that it was willing to prohibit the employment of British subjects in its public and private shipping, which had been an obstacle in the way of reaching a solution with Britain.

The offensive Orders-in-Council which had authorized the "paper blockades" were repealed almost simultaneously with our declaration of war. The textbooks commonly say that if there had been an Atlantic cable the war would never have come. No one knows whether this is true or not, since the British had made no concession on the impressment question. I have been intrigued with the negotiation which continued between the two countries *after* the declaration of war.

Our minister to Great Britain, William Pinkney, had returned to the United States in the spring of 1811, leaving his post in the hands of *chargé d'affaires* Jonathan Russell. At the time of the declaration of war, our State Department authorized Russell to make contact with Viscount Castlereagh, the British Foreign Minister. This he did, and was treated rather cavalierly by Castlereagh, who questioned Russell's powers to negotiate. On the matter of impressment Castlereagh was as adamant as ever, expressing surprise that the Americans should demand that the British government should desist from its "ancient and accustomed practice of impressing seamen from the ships of a foreign state." Russell had given Castlereagh his word that if the British would desist from impressment, the Americans, on their part, would agree not to allow British seamen to be employed on any of their ships. Castlereagh was unmoved, and in spite of repeated efforts Russell made no progress.

Another series of events, which took place after the war began, is not, I think, generally known. The British minister to the United States, Augustus Foster, left for home when war was declared. On reaching Halifax he learned of the revocation of the Orders-in-Council and felt, naturally enough, that if this action had come sooner that war would have been avoided. He thought, even so, that an armistice might be arranged. He made contact with General Dearborn on the Niagara frontier and on Foster's assurances Dearborn persuaded himself that an armistice should be declared. So from August 9th to 29th, the very period when General Hull was in greatest need of help, Dearborn was inactive. When Madison learned of this he wrote bluntly to Dearborn to the effect that Dearborn had no authority to declare an armistice when it was the intent of the government to prosecute a war. Generals have been dismissed for less.

A plea for an armistice was lodged in Washington by a more responsible officer. Admiral Sir John Borlase Warren, who commanded the British fleet in American waters, was authorized by the British government to open negotiations for an armistice based primarily on the revocation of the Orders-in-Council. Nothing was said in regard to impressment. I believe that Secretary Monroe's reply to Warren is worth quoting: "If the British Government is willing to suspend the practice of impressment from American vessels on the consideration that the United States will exclude British seamen from their service, the regulations by which this compromise should be carried into effect would be the sole object of negotiations. The armistice would be of short duration. If the parties agreed, peace would be the result, if negotiations failed each would be restored to its former state and all of its pretention by recurring to war."[11]

Monroe's statement makes clear that impressment was the sole reason for continuing the war. Had the British government desired peace, it could have had it by removing this one obstacle. This is the opinion of Dr. Zimmerman, whose thorough study of the question goes far towards supporting the contention that impressment was the prime cause for the war.

Lest I commit that fault for which I have criticized others, let me be quick to say that whereas I would give a sizeable amount of weight to impressment as a cause, I would much prefer that all causes, whether of great or little weight, should be included in any study of the question: that these causes be listed and weight assigned to them according to the judgment of the historian. I plead, then, simply for a full statement and a full analysis.

That the declaration of war was badly timed, I feel certain; that the war was badly fought, I feel even more certain. I am not ready to concede that the declaration was without justification, however unwise such a measure proved to be.

In this country the war was followed by a curious period in which there appeared a feeling of national unity; something of the same sort seems to have happened in Canada. Some writers have explained this new national enthusiasm on both sides of our boundary as an aftermath of the war. One might well be cautious, however, lest he fall into the *post hoc* trap.

Although it is not within the scope of this chapter to discuss the war and its outcome, yet I cannot resist speaking of a great event which took place not long after the war. When the sesqui-centennial of the Rush-Bagot Agreement occurs, that in my mind will be an occasion not only for commemoration but for real celebration, a celebration in which I hope all of us may have a share.

NOTES

1. *History of the United States,* 9 vols. (New York, 1889-91).

2. (New York: Harper and Brothers, 1902).

3. (March, 1924), X, 365-95.

4. (New York: Macmillan Co.).

5. Professor Utter was referring to a letter written by James Caldwell, to Worthington, Zanesville, Ohio, December 14, 1811. *Worthington Papers,* Ohio State Library, Columbus, Ohio. See also, Alfred B. Sears, *Thomas Worthington, Father of Ohio Statehood* (Columbus, 1958), p. 175.

6. *Expansionists of 1812,* p. 55.

7. "Nathanial Adams, to his brother, Detroit, August 9, 1812," Wisconsin State Historical Society. Quoted in Utter, *The Frontier State, 1803-1825* (Vol. 2 of *The History of Ohio,* ed. Carl Wittke, 6 vols.) (Columbus, 1942), p. 89.

8. "John Q. Adams to William Eustis, October 26, 1811," in Worthington Chauncey Ford, *Writings of John Quincy Adams* (New York, 1914), IV, 262.

9. *Impressment of American Seamen* (New York, 1925).

10. Richardson, *Messages and Papers of the Presidents* (Washington, 1917), I, 499-505.

11. "James Monroe to John Borlase Warren, October 27, 1812," *American State Papers: Foreign Relations,* III, 596.

SIR ISAAC BROCK:
THE HERO OF QUEENSTON HEIGHTS

W. Kaye Lamb

JUST OVER one hundred and fifty years ago, on December 2, 1811, Major General Isaac Brock, commander of the forces in Upper Canada, addressed a remarkable dispatch to his superior officer Sir George Prevost, Governor-in-Chief at Quebec. In it Brock outlined the course he proposed to follow in the highly probable event of war breaking out between Great Britain and the United States.

The likelihood of war was nothing new to Brock; the threat had been in the air ever since he had come to Canada, nearly ten years before. His only home leave, taken in 1805-06, had been cut short because (in his own words) "intelligence from the United States" had seemed to be "of so warlike a character" that he felt it his duty to hurry back to Canada. And the whole of his ten years in Canada had been devoted to a prolonged, sustained effort to improve the state of its defenses, with the contingency of an attack from the United States constantly in mind.

He had found Canada, in 1802, virtually defenseless. As late as 1807 he considered Quebec to be "the only tenable post," and the troops available in the whole country were still so few that, even if they could all be mustered there, "the number would," in Brock's opinion, "be insufficient to ensure a vigorous defence." In the huge, sprawling wilderness of Upper Canada, far to the west, into which settlers were steadily flowing, the chance of any effective resistance seemed remote.

To that wilderness Brock himself was ordered suddenly in July, 1810. The assignment was neither welcome nor wholly unexpected. Writing to his sister-in-law, he remarked: "I mentioned in a former letter my apprehensions of being ordered to the Upper Province. I return this

17

moment from waiting upon Sir James [Craig, the Governor-in-Chief] who sent for me, to say he regretted he must part with me, as he found it absolutely necessary that I should proceed upwards without delay. . . . I shall probably begin my journey upwards in the course of a few days."

Uncertainty about the length of his stay added to Brock's vexation. "Unless I take up every thing with me," he explained to his sister-in-law, "I shall be miserably off, for nothing beyond eatables is to be had there; and in case I provide the requisites to make my abode in the winter in any way comfortable, and then be ordered back, the expense will be ruinous. But I must submit to all this without repining. . . ." As it turned out, with the exception of a few months in 1811, Brock was to spend the whole of the short remainder of his life in Upper Canada.

It was not an unfamiliar land to him, as he had been posted for a time at York, and later at Fort George, in 1803-04; and although its remoteness depressed him, he was quick to acknowledge its attractions. "I have been as far as Detroit," he wrote to his brothers in September of 1810, a few weeks after his arrival at York, "a delightful country, far exceeding any thing I had seen on this continent." And the quiet life that his surroundings compelled him to live brought out aspects of his character that we might otherwise know little about. Thus in a letter written to his brother Irving from Niagara in January of 1811, we find him discussing the unlikely subject of books and reading.

"I hardly ever stir out," he wrote, "and unless I have company at home, my evenings are spent solus. I read much, but good books are scarce, and I hate borrowing. I like to read a book quickly, and afterwards revert to such passages as have made the deepest impression, and which appear to me most important to remember—a practice I cannot conveniently pursue unless the book is mine. Should you find that I am likely to remain here, I wish you to send me some choice authors in history, particularly ancient, with maps, and the best translations of ancient works. . . . As I grow old, I acquire a taste for study. I firmly believe that the same propensity was always inherent in me; but, strange to tell, although many were paid extravagantly, I never had the advantage of a master to guide and encourage me."

The man who wrote these words, and pictured himself as an elderly bookworm, was actually a vigorous, powerfully-built man of action, aged forty-one. Born in Guernsey in 1769 (the same year that saw the birth of both Napoleon and Wellington), he had entered the British Army as a lad of fifteen. Some years later he exchanged into the Forty-ninth Regiment, and with it he saw action in Holland in 1799.

Two years later the Forty-ninth was one of the units that took part in the famous attack on Copenhagen, under Nelson. By the time the Regiment was ordered to Canada, in the spring of 1802, Brock had for some years held the rank of Lieutenant-Colonel, and was its commanding officer.

He was soon deeply involved in the many things that had to be done if the military defenses of Canada were to be improved. Morale was at a low ebb; desertions were frequent; fortifications were run-down; the supply of arms was insufficient; the militia in many places existed only on paper; relations with the Indians were uncertain. It is indicative of the state of affairs that, in 1806, when Brock found himself temporarily in command of the forces in both Upper and Lower Canada, he discovered that the books of the commissary-general's office were in great confusion. In November, he was compelled to report to London that the deputy commissary-general's store account had not been examined since 1780, that the "account for fuel" was "likewise in arrear since . . . 1796, and the account of provision since . . . 1800."

It is a measure of Brock's quality that he was not discouraged. He tackled the problem of discipline and desertion with both vigor and imagination. Men under him discovered quickly that they could depend upon fair treatment, and that he was prepared to do battle on their behalf if regulations were totally unsuited to conditions and the climate. Clothing was a case in point. "Every man," Brock wrote in 1807 from Quebec, "is provided with a great coat agreeably to his majesty's regulations; but as the great coat is necessarily worn on all occasions six months in the year, it cannot by the strictest economy be made to last the specified time." He recognized the great temptations to desert that were offered by a country in which land was cheap and opportunity beckoned from many quarters. And always, just beyond the border, never far away, lay the United States. Brock came to the conclusion that the only solution was to settle reliable discharged army veterans in the country; their holdings would give them a vested interest in its safety and welfare, and their military experience would make them invaluable in the militia in time of war. Meanwhile, in Colonel William Wood's phrase, he "was strict, just, and kind"; and he had his reward. Discipline improved markedly, and desertion was rare in the units with which he had personal contact.

The problem of strengthening the militia was greatly complicated by the character of the population, particularly in Upper Canada. There the original settlers had been United Empire Loyalists, but in recent times many other settlers had streamed into the country, most of them from the United States, and their allegiance was, to say the least, uncertain. Many of the local militia units barely existed, and in some instances their arms had disappeared. It took time and patience to mend matters, but Brock devoted both to the task, and by 1812 the state of the militia had considerably improved.

Relations with the Indians were a vital factor in the defense of the country, and here again Brock labored patiently to improve matters. There is little evidence to suggest that he or any other responsible authority in Canada sought to rouse the hostility of the Indians against the United States; the aim was rather to try and make sure that, in the event of war, the natives would not be on the other side. Settlers feared them, and few things were more demoralizing than the possibility of Indian attacks and atrocities. It was customary to send gifts to the various chiefs at certain seasons of the year, and time and again Brock in his dispatches emphasized the importance of making the gifts generous, and of delivering them promptly, at the appointed time.

In retrospect, it is clear that both his character and his striking physique contributed greatly to the success of Brock's dealings with the Indians. The supreme example of this was, of course, his meeting in 1812 with Tecumseh, now recognized as the greatest of all Indian chiefs. Brock and Tecumseh instantly recognized each other's qualities, and their relations were marked by trust and high regard. Tecumseh gave Brock certain of his personal possessions that he must have valued highly, and two at least of these have survived—a sash, now in the museum of the Public Archives of Canada, and a ceremonial tomahawk that is a treasured relic in the hands of a distant kinsman of Brock's, in Guernsey.

The long frontier for which Brock was responsible extended from Lake Superior to Kingston, and consisted essentially of four immense lakes, with three narrow stretches of land between them. About the lakes themselves, I need say little; first, because the naval history of the War of 1812 is the subject of another chapter, and second, because the naval war did not become a serious factor until after Brock's death. But he was very much aware of the vital importance of controlling the lakes, and he commented from time to time in his letters and dispatches upon the many things that would have to be done if British command of them were to be assured.

Meanwhile, his first concern was with the military posts on both sides of the border. A little British fortification on St. Joseph's Island, between Lake Superior and Lake Huron, had its American counterpart at Michilimackinac, at the entrance to Lake Michigan.

Between Lakes Huron and Erie, Amherstburg on the Canadian side was countered by Detroit. Both countries had several posts in the Niagara area, notably Fort George and Fort Niagara, which stood on opposite sides of the entrance of the Niagara River into Lake Ontario. Queenston, with its heights, was upriver on the Canadian side, some seven miles from Fort George. Kingston, at the eastern end of Lake Ontario, looked across the water to Sackets Harbor, which, like Kingston itself, was an important naval base and shipbuilding center. As we shall see, Brock appreciated fully the threat it offered to British control of the lake.

In the last months of peace, Brock's life was complicated in two ways. In September of 1811, Sir George Prevost, a new military commander and Governor-in-Chief, arrived at Quebec to succeed Sir James Craig; and in October, with the departure of Lieutenant-Governor Gore, Brock was named administrator and president of the Government of Upper Canada. To his military duties there was thus added responsibility for the civil affairs of the province.

Whether Brock and Prevost had ever met, we do not know. If we may judge from the careful formality of Brock's communications, it seems unlikely. And if Brock had been at all well acquainted with Prevost's character and opinions, he would perhaps have modified some of the passages in the remarkable dispatch that he directed to the Governor-in-Chief on December 2, 1811. For in this dispatch Brock commented upon the probability of war with the United States, and took the view that the only hope for Canada lay in prompt attacks upon some of the American military posts in the small land areas that separated the Great Lakes. American superiority in population and material wealth was overwhelming, but it would take some time to organize an effective attack on Upper Canada, and in the interval Brock hoped that his small but well-disciplined force of regular troops, supplemented by militia and the Indians, could make itself felt.

The first essential, he told Prevost, was a striking success in the west that would impress the Indians and bring them firmly to the British side. With this in mind he hoped to be able to seize both Michilimackinac and Detroit. Each was garrisoned by only a few score men; but Brock surmised (correctly, as it proved) that Detroit would be quickly reinforced if war broke out. And he hoped that a victory at Detroit would impress not only the Indians but the militia and people of Upper Canada, about whose morale and loyalty he was deeply concerned. In the Amherstburg region, he reported, both the militia and the Indians "are now impressed with a firm belief, that in the event of war they are to be left to their fate." Of the Niagara area, which he expected to be the scene of the main American attack, he wrote: ". . . I cannot conceal from your excellency, that unless a strong regular force be present to animate the loyal and to control the disaffected, nothing effectual can be expected."

At this time Brock felt reasonably sure that he could count upon the support of the House of Assembly of Upper Canada, but another dispatch to Prevost, written two months later in February, 1812, shows how completely he had been disillusioned. "I had every reason," he wrote, "to expect the almost unanimous support of the two houses of the legislature to every measure the government thought it necessary to recommend; but after a short trial, I found myself egregiously mistaken in my calculation." Amendments to the Militia Act that Brock deemed to be essential were defeated, and his request for the suspension of *habeas corpus* was refused. "The great influence which the numerous settlers from the United States possess over the decisions of the lower house is truly alarming," he wrote to Prevost, "and ought immediately, by every practical means, to be diminished." The following month he was to comment on the doings of "Mr. Willcocks [a member of the Assembly] and his vile coadjutors"—with perfect justice, as events proved, for Willcocks later joined the Americans, raised a force of so-called Canadian Volunteers, and was killed in action at Fort Erie.

The declaration of war was approved by the Senate and House of Representatives in Washington on June 18, 1812. Brock heard the news on the 24th, but five weeks seem to have passed before he received any word from Prevost. In the interval, Brock had sent word to Captain Roberts, at St. Joseph's Island, instructing him to seize Michilimackinac. A few days later the order was modified, leaving the matter to Roberts' discretion; but the latter shared Brock's view that a sudden descent upon Michilimackinac might well be successful, and so it proved in practice. Roberts and his little band of regulars, supported by a motley crew of fur traders and Indians, appeared before the American post on July 17, and it at once surrendered.

This small event in the wilderness had the effect upon the Indians that Brock had anticipated; to an extent quite unjustified by the action, it convinced the Indians that the British could and would resist invasion. What Brock had not foreseen was the reaction of his commander-in-chief. Prevost, he discovered, was in reality opposed to aggressive action of almost any sort, and proposed to conduct the war purely on defensive lines.

Even at this late date it is difficult to judge Prevost fairly and accurately. It is clear that he regarded the War of 1812 as unnecessary, which it was, and in its early stages he clung stubbornly to the hope that military operations on any large scale could be avoided. He had been born in New York, and his many contacts with the United States may account for the reluctance that he showed on various occasions to press an attack with decision and energy. But there were other factors of a less personal nature. The votes on the declaration of war in the Senate and House had been far from unanimous; it was obvious that the war was highly unpopular in large and important sections of the country. The first essential, in Prevost's view, was to avoid doing anything that might antagonize the Americans, and thereby bring about the national unity that was so clearly lacking. On July 8, a member of Prevost's staff noted in a dispatch to Brock that the Governor's policy was "forbearance, until hostilities are more decidedly marked." And two days later Prevost himself elaborated the point when writing to Brock:

"Our numbers would not justify offensive operations being undertaken, unless they were solely calculated to strengthen a defensive attitude. I consider it prudent and politic to avoid any measure which can in its effect have a tendency to unite the people in the American States. Whilst disunion prevails among them, their attempts on these provinces will be feeble; it is, therefore, our duty carefully to avoid committing any act which may, even by construction, tend to unite the eastern and southern states, unless, by its perpetration, we are to derive a considerable and important advantage."

Before he received this dispatch, events had centered Brock's attention upon the second post that he had marked for capture—Detroit. As expected, it had been heavily reinforced, and General William Hull, who had served in the Revolutionary War and until recently had been Governor of Michigan, had arrived to take command. On July 12, Hull ferried a considerable force across the river and occupied the town of Sandwich, on the Canadian side. There he issued a proclamation to the inhabitants of Canada, in which he promised them protection of their "persons, property, and rights," and, in the name of the United States, offered them "peace, liberty, and security. Your choice," the proclamation added, "lies between these and war, slavery and destruction. Choose, then, but choose wisely . . . ."

There was some delay in sending news of the American invasion to Brock, but it caught up with him at Fort George, and he hurried at once to Amherstburg. There he issued a counterproclamation, on July 22; but in spite of its confident tone, he was in fact gravely concerned about the course of events. Hull's proclamation had had a considerable effect; Brock admitted in a dispatch to Prevost that "a general sentiment prevails that, with the present force, resistance is unavailing," and he assumed that Prevost would not be able to send him reinforcements. We have come, in fact, to the gravest crisis in Brock's defense of Canada.

Into this gloomy picture there strides suddenly the tall figure of Tecumseh; on August 5, Tecumseh attacked a small American force near Brownstown and captured some of General Hull's dispatches and correspondence. When Brock saw these papers, he was struck by their despondent and pessimistic tone. Convinced that bold action might well win the day, he gathered his modest forces and prepared to take the offensive. Meanwhile, his analysis of the situation had been confirmed by Hull himself, who had become alarmed by reports that Brock was preparing to oppose him, and had taken most of his men back across the river to the American side. Advancing to Sandwich, which the Americans had abandoned, Brock startled Hull on August 15 by sending him a summons to surrender. "The force at my disposal," Brock's letter began, "authorizes me to require of you the immediate surrender of Fort Detroit." Hull refused, but the next day, when Brock took his forces across the river and advanced on the fort, Detroit capitulated.

Hull is as difficult to judge as Prevost, and the final word may never be said about either of them; too much depends upon one's own point of view. Hull certainly showed little in the way of courage or resolution, in spite of the fact that his forces far exceeded Brock's in number. But his men were largely inexperienced and poorly-disciplined militia; the Indians were cutting his lines of supply and communication, and it would have been most difficult for him to sustain an effective resistance. He was getting old and timid, and had little desire to fight a pitched battle.

Hull's surrender caused a great outcry in the United States, and eventually he was court-martialed—a distinction which, by a strange turn of events, he was to share with Prevost. Hull was condemned to be shot, but the sentence was not carried out because of his age and the services he had rendered in an earlier war. Prevost, ordered to appear and explain his conduct in the later actions at Sackets Harbor and Plattsburg, died just before the court martial was to convene.

The results of Brock's victory at Detroit were even greater than he had anticipated. Michilimackinac had won the firm support of the Indians; Detroit had an electrifying effect upon the militia and the people of Upper Canada. It proved that the country could be defended, and that, in spite of vast superiority in material and numbers, an American invading force could be checked and even driven back. Defeatism, which had been rife, disappeared, and Upper Canada began to look with some confidence to the future.

Brock's personal opinion of the capture of Detroit was expressed in a letter to his brothers. "Some say," he wrote on September 3, "that nothing could be more desperate than the measure; but I answer, that the state of the province admitted of nothing but desperate remedies. I got possession of the letters my antagonist addressed to the secretary of war, and also of the sentiments which hundreds of his army uttered to their friends. Confidence in the general was gone, and evident despondency prevailed throughout. I have succeeded beyond expectation."

Brock felt, too, that Detroit was proof of the soundness of the general strategy he had worked out before the war. Now his great desire was to get on with the next step in the campaign as he conceived it. An attack on Sackets Harbor is not specifically mentioned in his dispatch of December 2, 1811, but there is a clear implication that an attempt should be made to seize the base and destroy the shipbuilding yards there. This plan Brock now set about carrying into effect. The day after he wrote to his brothers, he arrived in Kingston, full of plans for the new expedition. But at Kingston disturbing news awaited him. He found that Prevost, who was still laboring under the delusion that the war could be kept within bounds, had concluded an armistice with the Americans; and even though it was known that hostilities would soon be resumed, Prevost nevertheless refused to let Brock advance against Sackets Harbor. Thwarted in this way, Brock returned at once to Fort George. He had always been convinced that the major American effort at invasion would be made through the Niagara peninsula, and by the time he arrived on the scene it was evident that an attack was imminent.

Brock was faced with the usual predicament of a defender—the necessity of scattering his troops along a front of considerable length, so as to provide some sort of defense everywhere, whereas the invader was free to concentrate his forces at some chosen spot. And he labored under the added handicap of a strict injunction from Prevost to "refrain as long as possible . . . from every hostile act. . . ." No probing patrols could be organized, and no bombardments from across the river were to disturb the Americans.

Brock expected that the attempt to cross the Niagara River would be made near its mouth, not far from Fort George. The crossing was actually made at Queenston, seven miles upstream. The sound of heavy cannonading, which Brock heard from Fort George early on the morning of October 13, was the first intimation that something was afoot. Brock at once mounted his horse and rode to Queenston, where he discovered that a considerable American force had not only succeeded in crossing the river, but had captured a segment of Queenston Heights. The first essential seemed to be to dislodge them from this commanding position and, if possible, to retake the guns that had fallen to them. Rallying the available forces, Brock placed himself at their head, and led an advance up the hillside. His tall figure made him conspicuous, and only moments later he was struck by a bullet and fatally wounded.

It may be said that his death was in keeping with the Brock tradition; the history of the family is full of military tales in which the stalwart figure of a Brock was conspicuous in action. In the battle of Egmont-op-Zee, in 1799, the first important engagement in which Brock took part, his younger brother Savery was also engaged, as a fellow member of the Forty-ninth Regiment. Savery became involved in a furious battle for possession of a sand hill, and a young Irishman in the Regiment told later how he saw him "passing from the top of one sand hill to another, directing and encouraging his men. . . . Not doubting but that great numbers of the French soldiers would be continually aiming at him—a large man thus exposed—I watched from moment to moment to see him fall, but for two hours, while in my view, he remained untouched." Savery was lucky at Egmont-op-Zee; but at Queenston, Isaac was not. Savery, indeed, was to live for another forty-five years after this escape in battle; but the toll that war and accident and disease were apt to take in those days is well illustrated by the history of the Brock family. Isaac was one of ten brothers, eight of whom lived to maturity; but when Savery died in 1844 an entire branch of the family died out.

It is a measure of Brock's greatness that his death was not the end of the Brock story. His loss was a shattering blow to his troops; to the people it was an occasion for national mourning. But it is significant that his army survived his loss. Reinforcements hurried to Queenston, as he had planned that they should do; a British force worked its way carefully around the American position on the heights and attacked it from the rear; well-directed fire caused the flow of American troops across the river to drop to a trickle; and the day ended in a famous victory and the taking of over nine hundred prisoners. The difficult amalgam of regular forces, militia and Indians that Brock had contrived to achieve stood the strain, and continued to do so during the two years of war that lay ahead.

In retrospect, it is clear that the plans and preparations that made effective Canadian resistance possible in 1812 were Brock's work. The dispatch of December 2, 1811, outlined the course of action that he actually followed, and events proved that he had foreseen circumstances and probable events with amazing accuracy. What he had not foreseen was the handicap of a Governor and Commander-in-Chief who was to hamper him at every turn. But without actually disobeying orders, Brock contrived to carry out all his major projects, except the attack on Sackets Harbor, in spite of Prevost. One is tempted to recall that he had been at Copenhagen with Nelson, and that he must have taken careful note of the Admiral's famous demonstration of the usefulness of a blind eye.

Finally, it is noteworthy that Brock, a military figure, was long remembered by the general public—an unusual tribute in most democracies. Twelve years after his death, in 1824, when his body was moved from Fort George to the monument that had been built in his honor at Queenston, a vast crowd assembled; and in 1840, when the tall column was dynamited by a fanatic, another great crowd gathered to express their indignation at the act, and their determination to replace the shaft.

These people recognized that Brock had had a major share in Canada's survival in 1812. It is probably an exaggeration to say that if there had been no Brock there would now be no Canada; but there is sufficient doubt on the point to make it a reasonable topic for discussion.

THE CONTRIBUTION OF THE
CANADIAN MILITIA DURING THE WAR

George F. G. Stanley

I

THE PRINCIPLE that the male population of a country owes military service to the state in times of war has roots deep in Canadian history. In the seventeenth century, in the early years of the *Ancien Régime,* Louis XIV informed Governor Courcelle that steps should be taken to organize militia companies in the various parishes, to appoint officers to command them, and to assemble the men monthly for drill. Some years passed before these instructions were put into effect. However, in 1673, Governor Frontenac appointed captains of militia in each parish and issued orders that all male inhabitants between the ages of sixteen and sixty were liable for military duty, excepting only the clergy and those who held administrative appointments under the government. From that date until the capitulation of Montreal, eighty-seven years later, the militia played an important role in the defense of New France. Canadian militiamen became adept in all the arts of bush warfare—"la petite guerre" the Canadians called it—where initiative and mobility were the principal requisites. It was only as the fighting between France and Great. Britain became a matter of formal encounters between European-trained regulars during the Seven Years War, that the militia, lacking equipment, training and discipline, was relegated to a secondary position in Canadian defense.

Immediately following the cessation of hostilities in 1760, the victorious British disarmed the militia. Nevertheless, it was not long before they recalled the splendid efforts the Canadians had put forth in'times past, and when Pontiac rose in protest against the encroachments of the white man, an effort was made to enroll Canadians in the force that was assembled to suppress him. The Canadians, much to the annoyance of the British, came forward but slowly; and Governor

Murray threatened to have recourse to the old French militia laws if the necessary numbers were not forthcoming.[1]

During the American Revolutionary War, the Canadians were again called upon for assistance. On this occasion, Governor Guy Carleton looked to the seigneurs for help. Service on the basis of military land tenure had never been a feature of Canadian feudalism, and if few Canadians showed much enthusiasm for giving their lives for George III, it was because Carleton had missed the essential feature of the old militia system, that it was based upon the parish and the captain of militia, and not upon the seigneur and the seigneury. Canadian militiamen were, however, among the troops who defended Quebec against Montgomery and Arnold in 1775-76, and who struck southwards towards the Hudson under General Burgoyne in 1777.[2]

With the successful conclusion of the American rebellion in 1783, the British were faced with the problem of defending the frontier which the Treaty of Paris had created. Regulars could be provided from Great Britain to man the defenses of Canada; but what about the Canadians themselves? Following the precedent of the *Ancien Régime,* the British undertook to raise provincial regiments in the several British North American provinces, and to reconstitute the militia. In 1787 the Council of Quebec adopted a militia law which Carleton, now Lord Dorchester, believed would "have the effect of curing the dangerous supineness produced by the disuse of all militia service to train up youth in discipline and obedience, and to teach the people that the defense of the country is their own immediate concern. . . ."[3] A general enrollment of the militia was undertaken which showed, in that portion of Canada which is now Ontario, a strength of thirty-four hundred and ninety-two English-speaking and seven hundred twenty-one French-speaking officers and men.[4]

After the division of the old province of Quebec into two separate colonies, Upper and Lower Canada, in 1791, new militia laws were necessary. In Upper Canada, i.e., the region we call Ontario, the militia regulations were drafted by the Lieutenant-Governor, John Graves Simcoe, who followed English precedents. He divided the province into counties and over each he proposed to appoint a county Lieutenant, who would possess general oversight of the militia and who would enjoy the power of command or of recommending officers to command the county battalions or companies in their respective districts. Simcoe's ideas did not, however, take deep root in the uncultivated soil of Upper Canada, and the county Lieutenants never played the part in Canada that they played in England. The power to appoint to comissions remained in the hands of the Lieutenant-Governor without the intermediation of the county Lieutenants. As far as the rest of the scheme was concerned, it was little more than an enrollment plan, without provision for military training.

In Lower Canada, the militia laws, which were passed in 1793 and 1796, and again in 1800 and 1803, remained essentially those of the *Ancien Régime*. There were, thus, distinctions between the military service requirements of the two provinces; but they were the same in at least one fundamental, namely the practically universal liability for military service on the part of the male population, starting at the age of sixteen.

In 1807-08 the militia systems of both provinces were given a second glance under the threat of war with the United States. In Lower Canada orders were issued to call out one-fifth of the militia. The men were to be selected by ballot. As the tension eased, the Governor-General, Sir James Craig, who had served in Canada as a junior officer with General Burgoyne, did not proceed with the levy. The drafted force was excused from duty; although Craig did issue, on November 24th, 1808, a General Order lauding the Canadians for their loyal and heroic spirit in responding so readily to the draft.

In Upper Canada, at the same time, a new Militia Act was adopted, authorizing the movement of the militia out of the province, should it be necessary either to go to the assistance of Lower Canada, or to pursue an enemy "who may have invaded this Province," and also for "the destruction of any vessel or vessels built or building, or any depot or magazine formed or forming, or for the attack of any enemy who may be embodying or marching for the purpose of invading this Province."[5] An improvement in training was also aimed at, although the target was not a very difficult one. The law merely obliged officers to call out their companies not less than twice or oftener than four times a year for arms inspection and training.

As the possibility of war became more and more a probability, additional steps were taken to put the militia in shape to deal with the expected eventuality. Early in 1812 the legislature of Lower Canada authorized the Governor-General, Sir George Prevost, to embody some two thousand unmarried militiamen for three months, and in the actual event of war, the entire militia forces of the province should so drastic a step be necessary. Special financial appropriations were also made, and monies were placed at the Governor's disposal to be used should hostilities develop. Accordingly, on May 28th, twenty-one days before Madison's declaration of war upon Great Britain, Prevost raised four battalions of embodied militia and authorized the formation of a provincial regiment of *Voltigeurs* or light infantry, as a *corps d'élite*.

In Upper Canada, Isaac Brock, who had succeeded Lieutenant-Governor Gore as administrator of the province, prepared an appreciation of the defense situation in the Upper province as he saw it. In Brock's opinion, the militia of the upper St. Lawrence valley, from the Bay of Quinte to Glengarry, was "the most respectable of any in the province."[6] Elsewhere it was neither strong in numbers nor in enthusiasm. Along the Detroit frontier, in particular, it was weak and not very reliable. To improve the value of the militia as a fighting force, Brock proposed to introduce a new law providing for the selection of two companies from each militia regiment, to be known as flank companies, to be filled by volunteers between the ages of eighteen and fifty years, and to be "trained, exercised and instructed in military discipline" at least six times in every month. The remaining companies, the battalion companies as they were designated, were to be called out four times a year in peace time and monthly in war time. The strength of each flank company was limited to three officers, two sergeants, one drummer and thirty-five other ranks. Since uniforms were not available from the military stores, each man was to "provide himself with a short coat of some dark colored cloth made to button well round the body and pantaloons suited to the season, with the addition of a round hat." The officers were advised "on every occasion when in the field to dress in conformity to the men in order to avoid the bad consequences of a conspicuous dress."[7]

The proposals which Brock advanced were adopted by the legislature, but to his great disgust, several accompanying suggestions, such as oath abjuring all former allegiance to any other power, and for the suspension of *Habeas Corpus* when necessary, were rejected.[8]

In spite of the misgivings which plagued his mind following his encounter with the legislature, Brock went ahead with his plans to train the flank companies and to organize *ad hoc* militia cavalry, artillery and transport companies. "Printed rules and regulations for your future guidance are herewith forwarded," he wrote in letters to the officers commanding militia regiments, "The most simple and at the same time the most useful movements have been selected for the practice of the militia. . . . It is my earnest wish that the little the men have to learn may be acquired by way of a pastime and not looked upon in the light of an irksome restraint. The generality of the inhabitants, being already acquainted with the use of the musket, have the less to learn."[9] As he penned these words he knew that it would be upon the flank companies that he would have to rely, rather than upon the battalion companies: he knew, too, that many militiamen, particularly those in the townships of Burford, Oxford, Delaware and Westminster, in the western part of Upper Canada, were relatively recent arrivals from the United States, with no sense of loyalty either to the British crown or to the Canadian institutions.[10] Only in the counties where the Loyalist traditions were still strong, the Niagara peninsula, the Bay of Quinte, and Glengarry, the counties settled by the disbanded soldiers of the Loyalist corps, was the loyalty of the militia unquestioned. But if Brock was to use only the flank companies, they would yield, at first no more than seven hundred men, with the possibility of a maximum of eighteen hundred throughout the whole province once the flank company scheme was in full operation.[11] If Upper Canada was to be held for Great Britain, then Brock felt that there would have to be reinforcements of British regulars.

For the moment few regular reinforcements were available. The Governor-General, Sir George Prevost, was reluctant to send troops to the upper province. He warned his energetic subordinate to do nothing to provoke the Americans into attacking—perhaps the war clouds might be dispersed by the warm winds of appeasement blowing from London towards Washington—and made it clear that, if war should come, Montreal and Quebec and the lower St. Lawrence were the regions which would have to be held in strength. Brock would be obliged to manage as best he could in Upper Canada. The line of communications between Montreal and Amherstburg was too long, too thinly held, ran through areas inhabited by too many disaffected settlers—"doubtful characters," Brock called them[12]—to be defensible, even with such reinforcements as Prevost might be able to spare. The Governor's strategy was, therefore, to hold the fortress of Lower Canada, and let the upper province look after itself, with its one regiment of regulars, the Forty-first, its handful of Royal Veterans and gunners, its Newfoundland fencible unit and its Glengarry infantry just now recruiting, and its militia.[13]

II

The American plan of invasion was to strike at three widely separated points, Montreal, Niagara and across the Detroit River. Had these attacks been made simultaneously, or even had they been pushed with vigor and determination, it is hard to see how they could have failed to succeed. Yet fail they did. However, to say simply that the Americans neglected to make the most of their numerical superiority, or that their commanders showed a lamentable want of courage or judgment, is not enough. Some credit at least must be given to the men who defended their country in what were probably the most trying days of its history.

Oddly enough, Canadians have been disposed to poke fun at Henry Clay and those like him, who declared that the conquest of Canada would be a mere matter of marching. But, when we recall the large numbers of Americans settled in Western Upper Canada, and the insignificance of the defending forces in terms of numbers on the Detroit and Niagara frontiers, we can more readily understand why General Hull, who commanded the invasion force at Detroit, expected an easy victory. Lacking an adequate regular force to defend the long frontier from Cornwall to Amherstburg, Brock had no choice but to use his militia, however weak his faith in it may have been. Nevertheless, the response to his appeal for help from the militia was most gratifying. On the Detroit frontier the small British garrison at Amherstburg was promptly reinforced by the flank companies of the two Essex regiments. And when militiamen from Kent arrived, they and the Essex militia, commanded by Lt.-Col. Baptiste Baby, took up a position at Sandwich directly opposite Detroit. All told they numbered about four hundred and sixty officers and men.[14] However, with nothing to do but stand and watch the Americans preparing to attack them the militiamen began to lose their enthusiasm for military service: and when, in mid-July, General Hull launched his invasion and his proclamation, they could not conceal their anxiety to go home and forget about the war. Some even joined the invaders as the better part of valor. Colonel Matthew Elliott of the First Essex wrote to his friend, Colonel Claus at Niagara, that Hull's proclamation had "operated very powerfully on our Militia (who had come forward with as much promptitude as could have been expected)," with the result that "our Militia have left their posts and returned to their homes, so that . . . in two or three days we shall have very few of them at the post."[15] Not all the militia returned home. There were Canadian militiamen with Captain Muir when he occupied the line of the Canard River, four miles north of Malden. Detachments of Essex militia also took part in the skirmishes at Brownstown and Monguagon.[16]

Meanwhile, General Brock, aware of the very slow build-up of the enemy troops on the Niagara front, gathered reinforcements of regulars and militia from that region, and strengthened by militia detachments from Norfolk and Oxford, hurried to Amherstburg to take command of the troops facing General Hull. Expressing his "surprise" at the numerous desertions from the ranks of the Essex and Kent militia, and professing to believe that these were the product of "an anxiety to get in their harvests and not from any predilection for the principles or Government of the United States,"[17] Brock gathered together a force comprising three hundred regulars, four hundred militia together with six hundred Indians and crossed the Detroit River.[18] He was determined to compel Hull to come out from behind his defenses and fight. But Hull, who had previously withdrawn his troops from Canada, would not fight. And within a few hours the terms of surrender were agreed upon.

Brock's victory at Detroit gave a tremendous fillip to the morale of the people of Upper Canada. It also gave courage to the militiamen whose faith in victory had been at best, lukewarm. Moreover, it was now possible to give a large number of militiamen on the Detroit front leave to return home without incurring the stigma of desertion. A few militia, however, remained on duty with Procter at Amherstburg and took part in the several reconnaissance patrols up the Maumee River in September and October, 1812.

General Brock did not remain long at Detroit. He had to hurry away to meet the threat which was slowly developing under Van Rensselaer and Smyth on the Niagara River. Here the flank companies of the Lincoln militia had assembled, and together with some six hundred British regulars, had spent the summer watching the river from Fort George to Fort Erie. Approximately nine hundred militiamen were employed on guard duty in this region,[19] including, in addition to the infantry, a troop of dragoons raised by Alexander Merritt. A brief armistice, concluded by Prevost and Dearborn, made it possible for Brock to grant a few days' leave to the militia; but all too soon they were back again, reinforced by the flank companies from the Norfolk and York regiments. When the expected invasion finally did come on October 13th, the eight flank companies of the Lincolns and the flank companies of the Second York Regiment, Merritt's Dragoons and the Lincoln Militia Artillery, were all warmly engaged. Of the ninety-one officers and men killed and wounded in the fighting at Queenston Heights, no less than thirty-four came from the militia.[20]

It was anticipated that the Americans, with a substantial force of men at Buffalo, would make at least one more effort to cross the Niagara before the winter should set in. Accordingly drafts were ordered from the battalion companies to fill the gaps in the ranks of the flank companies, and also to strengthen the forces on the frontier. On this occasion, however, the response was apathetic. The inspiring figure of Brock was gone—he had been killed at Queenston Heights on October 13th—and the prospect of a long-drawn-out war with the United States was not an encouraging one. The disaffected element in the province, silent since the capture of Detroit, was becoming vocal again, and there were frequent reports of desertion from the militia. Finally, on November 28th, the Americans made their third effort to invade Upper Canada, this time from Black Rock. The attack, however, lacked even the impetus of the earlier one, and the invaders were hurled back by a much smaller force of regulars and militiamen, the latter drawn largely from the flank companies of the Norfolks and the Fifth Lincolns. The British loss was ninety-eight killed, wounded and missing. Of this total the two Norfolk companies and the Militia Artillery accounted for thirty-one.[21]

Military success, however, gave small comfort to the discontented militiamen. They were still, after many months, short of necessaries and were fed up with carrying out their military duties while lacking suitable clothing and shelter for themselves; others were worried about their wives and families. Desertions became more frequent as the weather became colder, even among those corps which had hitherto been noted for their reliability. It was in the hope of arresting this disposition to return home that the following Order was published on December 7th: "As the enemy must, in a short time, be compelled by the state of the river and the rigor of the season to suspend active operations, the Major-General hopes to enjoy soon the satisfaction of permitting the battalion companies, as well as a portion of the flank companies to retire to their homes. In the meantime, he recommends the most vigilant and spirited perseverance in the defense of this frontier to secure it from any immediate renewed effort of the enemy, and to preserve unsullied the reputation which the militia have acquired, in conjunction with the other troops, by their gallant and successful exertions."[22] When he wrote this Order, Sheaffe, who had succeeded to Brock's command in Upper Canada, knew what was behind the decline in morale. In a dispatch to Prevost he complained of the delays in forwarding supplies from Lower Canada. "The militia were therefore deprived of the early and extensive benefits which it had been intended to afford to them," he wrote, "and they were exposed to wants and privations which many bore for some time with commendable consistency. In their absence from their homes, their farms were suffering from neglect, much of their produce was lost and many of their families were in distress. This state of things caused desertions before the close of the campaign."[23]

Farther east at York and at Kingston, the response to Brock's initial call for volunteers had been in every way satisfactory.[24] It was believed that Kingston might be an early objective of the Americans, if only because of its position as the principal British naval base on Lake Ontario, and the militia of the Midland District gathered in force. With the non-appearance of the expected attackers, many of the militiamen were permitted to return home.

If there was little action at York and Kingston, there was more to be found along the banks of the St. Lawrence where the river formed the boundary between the two countries. On July 5th Colonel Richard Cartwright wrote from Kingston, to Sir George Prevost, "The militia of the several counties situate between this place and the Lower Province appear to be extremely well disposed and have made applications for larger quantities of arms and ammunition than we have to spare. They have been in part supplied and have been referred to Your Excellency for such further quantities as it may be thought expedient to furnish them."[25] A military headquarters for the Eastern District was set up at Prescott, and the militia of the counties of Dundas, Stormont and Glengarry and a troop of *ad hoc* dragoons, were given the task of escorting supplies between Montreal and Kingston and of establishing and guarding depots of arms and ammunition along the road. It seemed dull duty until September 16th, when an American force attacked a convoy of boats near Toussaint's Island. The fighting was sharp and the attackers were finally driven off by militiamen from the Dundas and Grenville county regiments.[26] Five days later another American force raided Gananoque, twenty miles east of Kingston.[27] A British counter-raid against Ogdensburg on October 4 was repelled by the American defenders; but on November 23rd, militiamen of the First Glengarry and First Stormont Regiments carried out a successful raid against the American post at Salmon River.[28] After a quiet period of two months the raids commenced again with Major Forsyth's attack upon a small detachment of Leeds Militia at Brockville.[29] Determined to put an end to the American capacity to carry out such raids, Lieutenant-Colonel Red George Macdonell of Glengarry, who had succeeded to the command at Prescott, prepared to strike a blow at Ogdensburg. On February 22nd, in mid-winter, with a force numbering six hundred and sixty-one, of whom three hundred and eighty-one were militia from the Eastern and Johnstown Districts, Macdonell drove Forsyth and his men away from the St. Lawrence. Macdonell described his exploit in this way, "In an hour after I assumed the command of my district, at the imminent peril of being punished for disobedience of orders, I attacked and drove the enemy from the frontier of the St. Lawrence, destroying his forts, flotilla, depots, etc. . . . thus removing the seat of war to five hundred miles from Montreal."[30]

III

Several months before the outbreak of war in June, 1812, General Brock had considered the formation of a volunteer militia battalion which would be embodied for a specified period of time.[31] Such a force would be more disposable than that usually available from the militia call-up. Nothing was done to carry out this proposal, however, until February, 1813, when it was put before the Upper Canada legislature by Major-General Sheaffe. The legislature adopted the proposal and funds were voted to provide a bounty of eight dollars for each man enlisting in the Volunteer Incorporated Militia Battalion.[32] The age limit for recruits was to be from sixteen to forty-five; it was expected that many of the men would come from those militia companies whose geographical locations did not give them an opportunity for active service. The new unit, although embodied for the duration of the war, was not a regular regiment. It was raised under and was subject to the militia laws of the province.

Regulations governing the organization of the new battalion were published in April. Little progress was made in filling the ranks, however, because the Americans resumed hostilities in the same month. The Canadian military authorities were too busy trying to solve the problems of invasion to be bothered with those of organizing and equipping and training a new unit. Under the emergency conditions imposed upon them by the enemy, they had recourse to calling up the flank companies and battalion companies of the sedentary militia to man the defenses of the province, just as they had done in 1812.

There had been ample warning during the spring of 1813 that the Americans were planning to take the initiative. On more than one occasion during the month of March, militiamen had been called out for duty on the Niagara frontier. But when the fighting did come in April it was not across the Niagara River, but against the provincial capital at York (now Toronto) that the enemy launched his attack. There is not much material available on the part played by the York militia in the action of April 27th; little more than the information that three York militiamen were killed and two were wounded in the fighting, and that two hundred and sixty-four officers and men of the First and Third York Regiments and the First Durham Regiment were made prisoners on the surrender of the town to General Dearborn.[33] During the brief period of American occupation a number of militiamen from the surrounding country gave themselves up to the victorious enemy; some at least did so in order that they might be paroled by the Americans and thereby escape responsibility for further military service during the campaign.

The loss of York seems to have cast a pall of gloom over the rest of the province. Just as militiamen everywhere had been elated by the British success at Detroit in the previous August, now they felt depressed by the American capture of the Upper Canadian seat of government. Perhaps the struggle to maintain their independence was not worth the effort; probably they would lose it in the end. An attitude of defeatism seems to have infected even the Lincoln regiments in the Niagara peninsula, although they were generally regarded as among the most reliable in the province. More and more did militiamen evince a reluctance to answer the call to arms. On May 19th Brigadier-General Vincent, who had succeeded to the command on the Niagara frontier after Sheaffe's withdrawal from York, wrote to Prevost, of the Lincoln county militia, "I can neither report favorably of their numbers nor of their willing co-operation. Every exertion has been made and every expedient used to bring them forward and unite their efforts to those of His Majesty's forces with but little effect, and desertion beyond all conception continues to mark their indifference. . . . ."[34] Only a stiff reinforcement of British regulars would restore their spirits and enthusiasm.

Nevertheless, the men of the First Lincoln Militia and the Lincoln Militia Artillery did turn out in force and fought well when Dearborn's troops, having given up York, landed near Fort George on May 27th. Charles Askin wrote to his father on June 2nd, "The Militia behaved as well as the Regular troops, many say better."[35] Unable to hold his position at Fort George and anxious to protect his communications with York and Kingston, Vincent called in his outposts on the Niagara frontier and retired along the escarpment in the direction of Burlington at the head of Lake Ontario. He did not take his militia with him. On June 4th he issued a General Order expressing his admiration for "the gallant conduct of that part of the militia which happened to be in the neighborhood of Fort George . . . whom the sound of cannon brought to aid us in repelling the common enemy," and giving them their release from military service until such time as "our reinforcements have all arrived and all other arrangements matured for repossessing ourselves of the country we have, for the moment, yielded. . . ."[36]

In spite of this formal release militia officers gathered squads of militiamen after the defeat of the Americans at Stoney Creek, and harried the retreating enemy as they pulled back towards Fort George along the shore road. These activities provoked reprisals on the part of the Americans. Arguing that by taking up arms the militia had nullified their civilian status, Dearborn issued orders that all Canadian militia officers in the areas controlled by the Americans should be seized and sent as prisoners-of-war to the United States. At the same time efforts were redoubled to parole as many militia other ranks as possible.

In this way it was hoped that the militia would be so weakened that it would prove of no further value to Brigadier Vincent. That the British felt the impact of this policy is apparent. When it was found that militiamen were using their parole as an excuse for refusing to work on the fortifications at Burlington, Sir George Prevost denounced "the unjustifiable practice" of the enemy "in paroling unarmed and peaceable citizens" and declared that such paroles could only "extend to military service in arms, either in garrison or in the field," and not to "performing their ordinary duties as subjects."[37] Vincent therefore made use not only of unparoled but also of paroled militia in building new field works at the head of Lake Ontario.

In the meantime, on the Detroit frontier, Procter had carried out several minor operations during the spring and early summer of 1813. Lacking any substantial reinforcements of regulars, he was obliged to supplement the British troops under his command with militiamen and Indians. Not only did he use militiamen of the two Essex regiments and the Kent regiment to furnish garrisons for the forts at Amherst-burg and Detroit, he also took them with him to Frenchtown in January, and on his expedition up the Maumee River against Fort Meigs early in May. On the latter occasion the militia component of his force numbered four hundred and sixty all ranks, a little over half of his total white force.[38] But, although Procter succeeded in defeating the American troops sent to relieve Fort Meigs, he could not take the fort itself, partly because his militiamen were anxious to return home to put in their crops, and partly because his Indians had no stomach for siege warfare. On May 9th, one of Procter's officers noted that the Indians and the militia had been "leaving us hourly, until our force was reduced to ten Indians, including Tecumsch, and very few of the Militia."[39] Understanding neither the mentality nor the needs of the militia under his command, Procter expressed his intention of never again using part-time soldiers if he could possibly avoid doing so. That he adhered to this resolution is proven by the complete absence of any reference to militia in his correspondence from this date until he was removed from his command after his defeat at the hands of General Harrison.

So alarmed were the British military authorities in Canada at the danger to Upper Canada implicit in Procter's defeat and Tecumseh's death at the Battle of the Thames on October 5th, that they contemplated not only the disbandment of the sedentary militia in western Upper Canada and the Niagara peninsula, but even a withdrawal as far east as Kingston. What they feared was a combined push from Moraviantown and Fort George and the junction of the two

American armies at Burlington. These alarms, however, were dissipated when Harrison withdrew his force to Detroit, and the American regulars were withdrawn from Niagara to strengthen the army being prepared for an offensive against Montreal. The British were thus able, not only to reoccupy their old positions in the peninsula, and to recover Fort George, but even, before the year was out, to capture the American Fort Niagara and to carry out raids along the American side of the Niagara River as far as Buffalo.

Even if they did recover lost ground in Niagara, it was impossible for the British to afford the troops necessary to regain Amherstburg or to contemplate a repetition of Brock's success against Detroit. The western flank was thus left exposed, the defense of that region resting entirely in the hands of the militia. Harrison, apparently, had no thoughts of trying to occupy Canadian territory, and American offensive action in this theater of war was limited to raids carried out by Americans led by expatriate Canadians like Benajah Mallory and Andrew Westbrook. Usually the avowed object of these raids was to make prisoners of militia officers and to take possession of public property; all too often, however, they degenerated into marauding raids for loot and plunder. The activities of the raiders caused both alarm and resentment among the Canadians, and *ad hoc* militia groups led by militia officers like the two Bostwicks, Burwell, Ryerse, Medcalf, Rapelje and others, were mustered from time to time to repel the invaders.

Typical of the actions of this period of the war was Colonel Henry Bostwick's encounter with William Sutherland's raiders near the mouth of Nanticoke Creek in November.[40] Learning that the enemy had taken shelter in a house belonging to one John Durham, Colonel Bostwick made his way through the woods until he was near his destination. Then he divided his men into three groups, sending one to prevent the Americans from escaping by way of a road to the rear, and with the others approaching to surround Durham's house. Captain John Bostwick of the First Norfolks, seeing no activity about the house, entered it with one of his subalterns, but was wounded and made prisoner. Hearing the sound of gunfire Colonel Bostwick hurried forward and exchanged several sharp volleys with the Americans. In the end several Americans were killed and sixteen of them were taken prisoners. Five managed to escape, including Sutherland. Two of the prisoners, John Durham and George Peacock, were identified as Canadians. They were charged with treason, tried, convicted and hanged at Burlington in July, 1814. This episode, small as it was, became the subject of a General Order in which the militia generally was called upon "to observe how quickly the energetic conduct of

45 individuals has succeeded in freeing the inhabitants of an extensive district from a numerous and well armed banditti, who would soon have left them neither liberty nor prosperity."[41] Later in the same year, in November-December, Lieutenant Medcalf of the Second Norfolk Regiment, with a small party of volunteers from the Norfolk and Middlesex militia, and a party of the Canadian Light Dragoons, surprised a number of raiders at Thomas MacCrae's in Raleigh township in Kent county near the mouth of the Thames River, taking as prisoners three officers and thirty-six other ranks of the Twenty-sixth U. S. Infantry Regiment. Without the loss of a man Medcalf's party, going and coming, had covered over two hundred and fifty miles in a country where roads did not exist and in the stormy weather of the end of the year.[42]

Meanwhile a serious situation had developed along the St. Lawrence. There had been no fighting in this region since Macdonell's punitive raid against Ogdensburg. Indeed, it had been the principal duty of the militia guarding the frontier during 1813 to promote and assist trade between the people of the British provinces and those of Vermont and up-state New York. Foodstuffs were needed by the British commissariat; and the Americans seemed willing enough to supply them for a price, in spite of the heavy penalties imposed by an Act of Congress against trading with the British.[43]

Partly to put an end to this illicit commerce and partly to gain a decisive hold in British North America, a two-pronged attack was planned against Montreal in the autumn of 1813. One force, commanded by Wade Hampton, was to be directed along Lake Champlain and the Richelieu River; the other, under James Wilkinson, was to proceed down the St. Lawrence. The first broke down when Hampton, having turned aside to avoid a strongly held British position on the Richelieu, was halted in his flanking movement by Colonel de Salaberry. De Salaberry's command included both provincial regulars and militiamen from the First and Third Battalions of Select Embodied Militia, and from the sedentary militia of Beauharnois.[44] Wilkinson's force likewise suffered a reverse when its rear guard was defeated at Crysler's Farm on the St. Lawrence.[45] Wilkinson's defeat, coming on top of Hampton's withdrawal, put an end to the whole operation, and Canadians in eastern Canada were able to breathe freely, at least for another winter season.

IV

During the winter of 1813-14, both sides prepared for the campaign which would begin with the opening of navigation in the spring.

Anticipating another invasion of the Niagara peninsula, the Second Lincoln militia was overhauled, for it had suffered considerably in two years of fighting. More significant, however, was the completion of the organization of the Battalion of Incorporated Militia which, by June, was reported to be in a satisfactory state of discipline and efficiency.

The Americans crossed the Niagara River early in July. Fort Erie did not offer any serious resistance and the Americans quickly swung north towards their objective at Fort George. At Chippewa, on the level tract between Street's Creek and the Chippewa River, Major General Riall awaited them with the main British force in the peninsula. He felt reasonably confident of success, for reinforcements of British regulars had at last arrived in Canada in numbers sufficient to bolster the troops in Upper Canada. With Riall also were two hundred militiamen, mostly from the Second Lincoln Regiment. When the Americans took their position, Riall attacked. To his surprise the Americans did not give way, and in the stubborn fighting which followed over five hundred casualties were suffered by the British troops. Of these the Second Lincolns lost twelve killed, sixteen wounded and fifteen missing, or over twenty per cent of their numbers. The fact that these casualties exceeded in number those of the Eighth King's Regiment, one of Riall's regular battalions, is the measure of how closely the Lincolns were engaged in the battle.[46]

Following his defeat at Chippewa, Riall retired to Fort George. Here he was joined by additional regiments of regulars, both British and provincial, and by the Incorporated Militia battalion. Three weeks later, on July 25th, the two armies met again, at Lundy's Lane. This, the most hotly contested battle of the war, was largely a battle of regulars. And both lost heavily, there being over eight hundred killed, wounded and prisoners, on each side. The militia contribution, in terms of blood let and men lost, was not an insignificant one. If the handful of sedentary militia from the Lincoln, York and Norfolk regiments lost only twenty-two men, the Incorporated Militia, which went into the battle about three hundred strong, suffered one hundred and forty-two casualties, or almost half its strength.[47] Each side claimed Lundy's Lane as a victory: but the fact that the battle proved a check to the American advance towards Fort George and Burlington and ended the invasion plans for 1814 gave greater color to the British claim.

If the militia, at least the sedentary militia, played only a minor role at Lundy's Lane, it should, in all fairness, be noted that almost one thousand militia had been mobilized in Upper Canada in 1814 to meet the American invasion, and that nearly all the outposts throughout the peninsula, at Ten Mile Creek, at Beaver Dams, at St. David's and elsewhere, were manned by militiamen. That these militia troops were not inactive is clear from the remark made by an American officer in a private letter written in July, 1814: "The whole population is against us; not a foraging party but is fired on and not infrequently returns with missing numbers."[48]

With the American withdrawal after Lundy's Lane, the war, as far as the people of Upper Canada were concerned, was almost over.[49] And the same was true of Lower Canada, where, except for the Third Battalion Select Embodied Militia and the Canadian Chasseurs (a new corps made up of drafts from the various embodied militia battalions in Lower Canada), the troops who formed Prevost's invasion force against Plattsburg were British regulars.

Only in western Upper Canada did the militia of Norfolk, Middlesex and Oxford remain actively engaged, playing hide, seek and fight with American raiding parties. In May, 1814 Lieutenant-Colonel John Campbell led a force of eight hundred regulars and American militia through the southern part of Norfolk county, burning and looting as he went.[50] The timely appearance of the Canadian militia seems to have saved the courthouse and public buildings of Charlotteville and persuaded Campbell to return to the United States. Americans were not proud of Campbell's actions. "One of our citizens," wrote a resident of Erie on May 19th, "on his return, has richly furnished his house with looking glasses, china, plate, etc. I fear that in consequence of this destruction of private property, we may expect from the enemy similar treatment."[51] A court of inquiry was held into Campbell's conduct. It held that he was justified in destroying mills and distilleries since both contributed to the Canadian war effort with food and soldiers' comfort, but that in destroying private property and stealing private possessions he had gone beyond the approved conduct of an American officer, even if he did argue that the owners of the property in question had been "actively opposed to American interests in the present war."[52]

On September 1st Captain Rapelje, with a small number of Middlesex militia, successfully ambushed a party which the traitor Westbrook had led to Oxford Township. The elusive Westbrook, however, was riding in the rear and escaped by a path through the woods, much to the annoyance of the Canadians. And within a matter of weeks he was back again with a raid upon Port Talbot.[53]

The most formidable of the many raids carried out in western Upper Canada during 1814 was that commanded by Brigadier-General Duncan McArthur, who led a force of eight hundred Americans, equipped with cannon, from Detroit, over the St. Clair River, to the Thames at Moraviantown. His declared objective was Burlington. But when he found his advance blocked at the Grand River by a detachment of the Forty-first Regiment and militia levies from Norfolk and Oxford, and a group of Iroquois Indians, McArthur diverted his course towards Malcolm's Mills where he dislodged Lieutenant-Colonel Bostwick's militia on November 6th.[54] Then, hurrying towards the Thames, paroling militiamen and burning buildings as he went, he reached Detroit on November 17th. It was a remarkable exploit, for McArthur had travelled no less than six hundred and fifty miles in twenty-eight days, inflicted a defeat on the Canadian militia, destroyed five flour mills, and inconvenienced the British commissariat at scarcely any loss to himself.

V

So much for the story of the Canadian militia in the War of 1812-14. Did the militia play a significant part? Did militiamen prove of any real value to the country in the days of its travail? The answer to both questions is yes. Not the dominant role, it is true; but an important and essential role for all that.

During the three years of the war militiamen transported and convoyed military supplies; they provided garrisons for towns and depots; they constructed fortifications; they furnished guards at various points along the many miles of frontier between Amherstburg in the west and Lacolle in the east. These were necessary and important tasks. Even more important was their contribution of fighting troops. During the first year of the war, when the regulars in Upper Canada were few in number, militiamen were a large part, and usually the major component of the forces which defeated the enemy at Detroit, Queenston Heights, Frenchman's Creek, and Ogdensburg. Without the assistance of the flank companies and the battalion companies of the several Lincoln, Norfolk, Essex and York Regiments, the British would have been hard put to secure victory at any of these engagements. As more regulars, both provincial and British, became available for the defense of the country, the militia of necessity became less important as a component of the fighting forces; although the contribution of militiamen at Fort George, Frenchtown, Fort Meigs, Lacolle and Chateauguay in 1813 cannot with fairness be passed over lightly. Nor can we ignore the part played by the Incorporated Militia at Lundy's Lane or that of the Norfolk, Oxford and Middlesex militiamen in the defense of those regions west of Burlington in 1814.

Of course the militia had its weaknesses as a military force. It lacked training and it lacked discipline, although both of these drawbacks became less significant as militiamen gained actual experience under war conditions. Much more serious was the fact that the militia was not a disposable nor a permanent force; that militiamen, being soldiers only for several weeks or months during the year, kept one eye upon their farms and their families, and were disposed to go home when either of these interests demanded their attention. It was to overcome this weakness that Prevost embodied six battalions of militia in Lower Canada and that the Volunteer Incorporated Militia Battalion was formed in Upper Canada. Nevertheless, the various commanding officers in both Upper and Lower Canada recognized the worth of the sedentary militia and utilized its services in virtually every operation of the war. General Brock was speaking in a prophetic vein when he wrote Prevost several months before the war began, "Unless the inhabitants give an active and efficient aid, it will be utterly impossible for the very limited numbers of the military who are likely to be employed, to preserve the province."[55] That the province was preserved, proves both the activity and the efficiency of the aid rendered.

But if the militiaman left his mark in this fashion upon the history of Canada, he also left it in another. Out of the militia participation in the war grew the national myth of the loyal militiaman springing to arms in 1812 and saving the country from its forcible incorporation in the United States. It was too easy to forget the apathy, the hesitations, and the downright refusals to fight which occurred from time to time, and the desertions and the embarrassments caused by the need to give militiamen farm leave. It was easy to magnify the role of the militiaman in the victories of Detroit, Queenston Heights and Lundy's Lane. On the other hand, in more recent years, there is discernible a tendency, when defending the right of the British regulars to share in the glories of the war, to forget that without the support of the militia, both behind and in the lines of the fighting troops, the regulars in all probability would have abandoned Upper Canada to the invaders, and fought the war on the island of Montreal or below the cliffs of Quebec. Both British regulars and Canadian militia complemented each other. Neither without the other could have functioned as an effective or efficient military force. The honors of 1812 must be shared by Canadian militia and British regulars alike.

NOTES

1. G. F. G. Stanley, *Canada's Soldiers* (Toronto, 1961), p. 100.

2. G. F. G. Stanley, *For Want of a Horse, Being a Journal of the Campaigns against the Americans in 1776 and 1777 Conducted from Canada* (Sackville, 1961), pp. 23-24.

3. E. J. Chambers, *The Canadian Militia, the History of the Origin and Development of the Force* (Montreal, 1907), p. 30.

4. Districts of Lunenburg, 1525; Mecklenburg, 1141; Nassau, 600; Hesse (Detroit), 721 French and 226 British Militia. In 1805 the Militia enrollment in Upper Canada totalled 652 officers and 7947 other ranks.

5. "Militia Act 1808, clause 9," in E. A. Cruikshank, *The Documentary History of the Campaign upon the Niagara Frontier in the Year 1812* (Welland: Lundy's Lane Historical Society), p. 6.

6. "Brock to Prevost, 2 Dec. 1811," Public Archives of Canada, C 673.

7. "Record of the Services of Canadian Regiments in the War of 1812—The Lincoln Militia," in E. A. Cruikshank, *Selected Papers, 1903* (Welland: Canadian Military Institute, 1904), p. 19.

8. "Brock to Baynes, 12 Feb. 1812," in F. B. Tupper, *The Life and Correspondence of Major General Sir Isaac Brock, K. B.* (London, 1845), pp. 123-28.

9. Quoted from letter of Brock to Fraser, 8 Apr. 1812, "Record of the Services of Canadian Regiments in the War of 1812—The York Militia," in E. A. Cruikshank, *Selected Papers, 1908* (Welland: Canadian Military Institute), p. 32. See also "Brock to Prevost, 22 Apr. 1812," Public Archives of Canada, C 676.

10. Among the disloyal elements were Joseph Willcocks, who in 1813 organized a corps of deserters and refugees called "The Canadian Volunteers," with Andrew Westbrook, Benejah Mallory, Simon Watson and Ebenezer Allan. Willcocks was killed at Fort Erie, 4 Sep. 1814. For a report on these people see "Springer to Brock, 23 Jul. 1812," Public Archives of Canada, 688A.

11. "Brock to Prevost, 25 Feb. 1812, and 3 Jul. 1812," Public Archives of Canada, C 676.

12. *Ibid.*, "Brock to Prevost, 25 Feb. 1812." See also "Abstract of General Returns of Troops in Upper Canada under the Command of Major General Brock, 30 Jul. 1812," Public Archives of Canada, C 676. This return showed: Royal Artillery, 80; 10th Royal Veterans, 196; 41st Regiment of Foot, 1016; Royal Newfoundland Fencibles, 368. In Lower Canada the returns showed 8720 rank and file on duty, including regulars, embodied militia, sedentary militia and voyageurs.

13. *Ibid.*, "Prevost to Liverpool, 18 May 1812," C 1707.

14. *Ibid.*, "St. George to Brock, 8 Jul. 1812," C 676.

15. *Ibid.*, "Elliott to Claus, 15 Jul. 1812."

16. *Ibid.*, "Procter to Brock, 11 Aug. 1812." See also "Hull to the Secretary of War, 13 Aug. 1812," in E. A. Cruikshank, *Documents Relating to the Invasion of Canada and the Surrender of Detroit 1812* (Ottawa: Public Archives of Canada, 1912), p. 141.

17. *Ibid.*, "District General Orders, 14 Aug. 1812," p. 142.

18. "Brock to Prevost, 16 Aug. 1812," Public Archives of Canada, C 676. For the Prize Pay List, see Cruikshank, *Documents,* p. 148.

19. "District General Orders, 2 Jul. 1812," in Cruikshank, *Documentary History 1812,* pp. 91-92. See also "Brock to Prevost, 1812," Public Archives of Canada, C 676. Brock wrote, "The Militia which assembled here immediately on the account being received of war being declared by the United States have been improving daily in discipline, but the men evince a degree of impatience under their present restraint that is far from inspiring confidence. So great was their clamor to return and attend to their farms that I found myself in some measure compelled to sanction the departure of a large proportion. . . ."

20. "Return of Killed, Wounded and Missing at Queenston," Public Archives of Canada, Q 119. In addition to the figures quoted there were 21 missing, of whom 15 were militia.

21. "Return of Killed, Wounded and Missing, 21-28 Nov. 1812," in Cruik-shank, *Documentary History 1812*, Part II, p. 230. The losses were: 16 killed (militia, 2), 47 wounded (militia, 18), 35 missing (militia, 11).

22. *Ibid.*, "District Militia Order, 7 Dec. 1812," p. 286.

23. *Ibid.*, "Sheaffe to Bathurst, 31 Dec. 1812," p. 338.

24. "MacPherson to Freer, 5 Jul. 1812," Public Archives of Canada, C 676. Major MacPherson wrote, "I never saw men come forward with more cheerfulness or more willing to be instructed than the Militia of this and neighbouring districts."

25. *Ibid.*, "Cartwright to Prevost, 5 Jul. 1812." See also *Garrison Order Book, Kingston, Jul.-Aug. 1812*, R. M. C. Library.

26. "Heathcote to Vincent, 3 Oct. 1812," Public Archives of Canada, C 677.

27. *Ibid.*, "Memorial of Colonel Stone to Maitland," MG 23, H II. See also "Regimental Orders by Col. Stone, 23 Sep. 1812," II, RG 9, 1B1.

28. *Ibid.*, "Gray to Baynes, 23 Nov. 1812," C 729.

29. *Ibid.*, "General Orders, 25 Feb. 1813," 1203^1/$_0$ F. See also "Bruyeres to Prevost, 19 Jan. 1813," C 387. Bruyeres wrote, "a small troop of cavalry with a volunteer Rifle Company and some Militia" had been stationed at Brockville and "a good Post with a company of Militia" at Gananoque.

30. *Ibid.*, "Macdonell to Taylor, 18 Apr. 1826," Q 342. Out of total casualties numbering 8 killed and 52 wounded, the militia suffered 2 killed and 20 wounded, or rather less than half.

31. *Ibid.*, "Brock to Prevost, 25 Feb. 1812," C 676.

32. *Ibid.*, "Sheaffe to Prevost, 13 Mar. 1813," C 703. The bounty was raised to ten dollars owing to "the importance of forming without delay an effective force from the Militia" ("Sheaffe to Prevost, 15 Mar. 1813"). For details regarding the organization of the Incorporated Militia see Aeneas Shaw (Adjutant-General Militia), "Regulations, 18 Mar. 1813," C 1700.

33. *Ibid.*, "Terms of Capitulation, 27 Apr. 1813," C 695A. The surrender included 37 officers, 23 non-commissioned officers and 204 rank and file. See also "Sheaffe to Prevost, 5 May 1813."

34. *Ibid.*, "Vincent to Prevost, 19 May 1813," C 678.

35. "Charles Askin to his father, 2 Jun. 1813," *The John Askin Papers 1796-1820*, ed. Milo M. Quaife (Detroit: Library Commission, 1931), II, 754. See also "Vincent to Prevost, 28 May 1813," Public Archives of Canada, C 678. As against Askin's statement, Vincent wrote, "My sentiments respecting the Militia are already known, and it will not be supposed that their attachment to our cause can be steady under the peculiar complexion of the present times."

36. "Militia District General Order, 4 Jun. 1813," in Cruikshank, *Documentary History 1813*, Part I, pp. 301-02.

37. "Record of the Services of Canadian Regiments in the War of 1812—The Lincoln Militia," in Cruikshank, *Selected Papers, 1903*, p. 30. For correspondence re paroling and exchange of prisoners, see the Public Archives of Canada, C 689.

38. "Embarkation Returns of the Western Army on the Expedition to the Miami, 23 Apr. 1813," Public Archives of Canada, C 695A.

39. "Record of the Services of the Canadian Regiments in the War of 1812 —The

Militia of Essex and Kent," in E. A. Cruikshank, *Selected Papers, 1906* (Welland: Canadian Military Institute), p. 59. On May 14 Procter reported to Prevost that both the Indians and the militia had proved unreliable. Public Archives of Canada, C 1219.

40. "Bostwick to Glegg, 14 Nov. 1813," Public Archives of Canada, C 681.

41. "Record of the Services of the Canadian Regiments in the War of 1812 —The Militia of Norfolk, Oxford and Middlesex," in E. A. Cruikshank, *Selected Papers, 1907* (Welland: Canadian Military Institute), p. 52.

42. "Medcalf to Bostwick, 25 Dec. 1813," and "Drummond to Prevost, 25 Jan. 1814," Public Archives of Canada, C 682.

43. John Ross wrote to David Parish on 23 Jul. 1813, "It is incredible what quantities of cattle and sheep are driven into Canada. We can hardly get any for love or money; the day before yesterday upwards of 100 oxen went through Prescott, yesterday about 200." Quoted in H. F. Landon, *Bugles on the Border* (Watertown, 1954), p. 34.

44. "de Salaberry to de Watteville, 26 Oct. 1813," Public Archives of Canada, C 680.

45. *Ibid.,* "Morrison to de Rottenburg, 12 Nov. 1813," C 681. There were only a few militiamen with Morrison at Crysler's Farm. There were, however, about 300 Dundas and Glengarry militia with Major Dennis at Hoople's Creek opposite the American advanced guard. "Dennis to Scott, 10 Nov., 11 Nov. 1813," C 681.

46. "Riall to Drummond, 6 Jul. 1814," Public Archives of Canada, C 684. See also "Return of Killed, Wounded and Missing, 5 Jul. 1814." Three militia officers were killed and 4 wounded, almost one-third of the total officer losses. Drummond praised the conduct of the Second Lincolns in a report to Prevost, 10 Jul. 1814.

47. *Ibid.,* "Drummond to Prevost, 27 Jul. 1814."

48. *Ibid.,* "Riall to Drummond, 19 Jul. 1814." Riall wrote, "Almost the whole body of Militia is in arms and seems actuated with the most determined spirit of hostility to the enemy." See also "Major MacFarland, Twenty-third U. S. Infty to his wife," in Cruikshank, *Documentary History 1814,* p. 73.

49. After Lundy's Lane the majority of the militia was allowed to return home.

50. "Campbell to Riall, 16 Jun. 1814," Public Archives of Canada, C 684. See also "Talbot to Riall, 16 May 1814," and "Drummond to Prevost, 27 May 1814," C 683. In his letter Campbell wrote, "what was done at that place [Port Dover] and its vicinity was planned by myself and executed upon my own responsibility." Campbell was O. C., Eleventh Regt, U. S. Infty.

51. *New York Spectator,* 1 Jun. 1814. Quoted in G. Tucker, *Poltroons and Patriots* (New York, 1954), p. 422.

52. "Opinion of a Court of Enquiry Held at Buffalo, 20 Jun. 1814," in Cruikshank, *Documentary History 1814,* p. 18.

53. "Drummond to Freer, 5 Sep., 19 Sep. 1814," Public Archives of Canada, C 685.

54. *Ibid.,* "Bostwick to O. C. Long Point, 3 Nov. 1814," "Smith to de Watteville, 7 Nov. 1814," and "Drummond to Freer, 12 Nov. 1814," C 686.

55. *Ibid.,* "Brock to Prevost, 2 Dec. 1811," C 673.

NAVAL POWER ON THE LAKES, 1812-1814

C. P. Stacey

WRITERS OF TEXTBOOKS have often failed to make the War of 1812 comprehensible. The story emerges as a series of apparently disconnected naval and military episodes, lacking any visible pattern and making no particular sense. The war can be understood only through a mastery of simple but fundamental strategic elements which determined its course: the military and economic resources of the combatants; the nature of the respective lines of communication over which those resources had to be brought to bear; and, finally, the vital importance of naval power on the Lakes in deciding the outcome of events.

Few phases of naval history can be studied seriously without taking account of Admiral Mahan's theories on the influence of sea power upon history; and the war that took place on the inland seas of North America in 1812-14 is certainly not one of them. It is nearly sixty years since Mahan published *Sea Power in its Relations to the War of 1812;* but it remains probably the best book ever written about that war, and this curious episode in North American history would be better understood if more people had read it. This essay is not much more than a gloss upon Mahan's work. One can amplify the Admiral's account, one can even correct it here and there in some matters of detail; but its general soundness is beyond question, and the present-day student can only honor and admire it.

I

No one who has studied the question with any seriousness is likely to question the proposition that in 1812-14 the determining influence in military operations in the Great Lakes basin was naval power. It is worthwhile, however, to consider for a moment the reasons for its importance.

The defense of Upper Canada against the United States was primarily a problem in communications. Almost everything that made defense possible came from Great Britain. Personnel and material, naval and military, moved across the Atlantic and up the St. Lawrence in ships. From Montreal, the head of ocean navigation, men and equipment moved on by bateau or by the rough roads along the river bank to Kingston, the naval station at the east end of Lake Ontario. From there to the western posts, the highway was the Great Lakes themselves and their connecting waters and portages. The farther west a British naval vessel or a company of British troops operated, the longer and the more insecure became its line of supply. At Amherstburg, the little naval base at the western extremity of Lake Erie, British soldiers and sailors were out on a very long limb; at Michilimackinac, the post at the head of Lake Michigan captured at the beginning of the war, they were on the last twig.

Even in the best-settled parts of Upper Canada, roads were vile; only by water could men or goods be moved with ease and speed. The British forces defending Upper Canada were thus placed in a singularly uncomfortable position. Their fighting front—the frontier which they had to defend—and their all-important line of communication were in fact one and the same. In the old strategic phrase, they were "formed to a flank," with the whole length of their communications exposed. And the Americans had only to cut those communications to cause the whole of Upper Canada west of the point of severance to fall into their hands at an early date. The capture of Montreal would have given them the entire province, and they ought to have made Montreal their supreme objective from the beginning. Luckily for Canada, the United States government adopted a plan along these lines only after the Treaty of Ghent had been signed.[1]

In these circumstances, the importance of naval control of the Lakes is evident. If the British lost it, their communications were gone and with them went Upper Canada, or a good part of it. When their squadron on Lake Erie was destroyed in September 1813, the inevitable result was the loss not only of Detroit but also of the adjoining western region of Upper Canada, which remained in American hands until the end of the war. Lake Ontario was much more important than Lake Erie, simply because its more easterly position on the line of communication meant that a defeat there would give the Americans the whole central area of the province as well. This fact is reflected in the tremendous efforts which both sides exerted to gain and hold command of Lake Ontario in 1814. Control of that lake was necessary to a successful defense of the province, and equally necessary to the American offensive.

This raises the question of the American lines of communication. It is often forgotten that the ultimate bases for the American naval operations on the Lakes were the navy yards on the Atlantic seaboard. As British naval superiority on the Atlantic increasingly bottled up the United States ocean fleet, the resources of these yards became available to support the effort on the Lakes. As long as the American naval station for Lake Erie was Black Rock, near Buffalo, the New York navy yard had to concern itself with both that lake and Ontario; but when Commodore Chauncey moved the base to Erie, Pennsylvania, at the end of 1812, the Philadelphia navy yard could look after it, with some help from Washington. The New York yard could now concentrate upon Lake Ontario, and also give some attention to Lake Champlain.

Between Philadelphia and Erie, and between New York and Sackets Harbor (the American base for Lake Ontario), the communications were, by the standards of that day, comparatively efficient. There was good road connection between Philadelphia and Pittsburgh, and thence there was water transport by the Allegheny River and French Creek to within fifteen miles of Erie. From New York to Sackets there was the water route by the Hudson and the Mohawk to Rome, and onwards by a canal connecting with Wood Creek, Oneida Lake, and the Oswego River. The roads in the northern parts of New York and Pennsylvania were not good; but on balance the routes supplying the United States bases were better and shorter than those on the Canadian side. They were also far less exposed. Broadly speaking, they ran at right angles to the frontier, offering the British little opportunity for interrupting them. An exception was the final section of the water route to Sackets Harbor, which ran across the corner of Lake Ontario. The British struck at this route more than once, without great success.

The logistical side of the war has received less attention than it deserves. The industrial strength of Great Britain in 1812 was far superior to that of the United States. The United States, however, was far stronger than Canada. The United States could make its own guns, anchors and cables, but no such heavy war material was manufactured in Canada. When Commodore Chauncey was appointed to the American command on the Great Lakes, he sent to the Lakes from the New York navy yard a miscellaneous shipment of cannon and equipment. He reported, "The carriages have nearly all been made, and the shot cast, in that time [three weeks]. Nay, I may say that nearly every article that has been sent forward has been made." Admiral Mahan's comment on this is, "The words convey forcibly the lack of preparation which characterized the general state of the country."[2] This is perfectly true; but the admiral might have added that a nation which could produce such material, and produce it so rapidly, had a great advantage over a colony whose sole source of "warlike stores" was the metropolitan community on the other side of the Atlantic. The fact that these stores had to cross an ocean to reach Canada was not an important handicap as long as the Royal Navy's command of the sea was not seriously challenged; but the fact that all the supplies had to be dragged up the St. Lawrence rapids in boats posed a transport problem which grew steadily worse as the lake warships increased in number and size. In 1814, when ships of more than one hundred guns began to be built on Lake Ontario, this problem threatened to become insoluble.[3]

The American advantage was not due merely to the industries of the seaboard cities. Industry was beginning to spring up much closer to the lake theater of war, and the war itself accelerated the process. The iron industry was developing in western Pennsylvania. Historians have almost unanimously failed to notice the debt of Perry's Lake Erie squadron to the infant industries of Pittsburgh. That town doubled its population between 1810 and 1815, and it made Perry's galley stoves, cables, anchors, and shot. Perry was not grateful to the Pittsburgh ironmasters —his letters abuse them in the strongest terms for failing to meet the delivery dates they promised; but they produced the stuff in time for him to win his battle, and he could not have won without it. With Pittsburgh behind him, Perry was far better off than his opponent Barclay at Amherstburg, who had no local iron industry to rely on and was at the wrong end of a long and shaky line of communication running back to Montreal.[4]

II

Let us now consider the effect of these basic conditions on actual operations.

The naval situation on the Lakes at the beginning of the war was extremely advantageous for the British; they had a naval force there and the Americans had not. The British had been compelled to maintain government vessels on the Lakes, because it was only by water that troops and supplies could be moved with any ease. The Provincial Marine of Upper Canada was not part of the Royal Navy and was not organized as a fighting service; it was a transport service controlled by the Army. But its vessels were armed and were built on the lines of fighting ships, and more and larger ones were built as the war came nearer. The Americans made no such preparations. They did build a brig, the *Oneida*, on Lake Ontario in 1809, but she seems not to have been manned until 1811; and when war broke out in 1812 the British had complete naval command of the Lakes both above and below Niagara Falls.

Control of the water went far to make up for the smallness of General Brock's military force. It meant that his enemy was able to come at him only by land routes, while he himself could shuttle his little reserves rapidly back and forth along the menaced frontier of his province as the situation required. The tactical assistance of the Provincial Marine vessels was frequently very helpful; General Hull recorded that the British crossed the Detroit River to attack him "under cover of their ships of war."[5] This was one point where the American communications were exposed; the last sixty miles or so of Hull's supply line, as it ran back to the interior of Ohio, followed the shoreline of Lake Erie and the Detroit, and could easily be cut by waterborne British raids. Two detachments sent back by Hull to open the line of communication were intercepted by British troops and Indians. These conditions prepared the way for Hull's withdrawal from Canada and for his surrender. General Brock was an exceptionally able, bold, and energetic officer, but it is doubtful whether he would have been able to accomplish what he did in the summer of 1812 without the advantages conferred upon him by naval control of the Lakes.

This situation was short-lived. Before the year 1812 was out, the United States Navy had established itself effectively on the Great Lakes and was challenging the British command. Admiral Mahan wrote, "It cannot but be a subject of professional pride to a naval officer to trace the prompt and sustained action of his professional ancestors, who reversed conditions, not merely by a single brilliant blow, upon which popular reminiscence fastens, but by efficient initiative and sustained sagacious exertion through a long period of time."[6] When war broke out the United States had no naval bases and almost no ships on the Lakes. Within a few months, Captain Isaac Chauncey had set up the base at Sackets Harbor and created a squadron on Lake Ontario by taking up and arming merchant schooners to reinforce the *Oneida.* By November, 1812 he was strong enough to venture an attack upon Kingston, and claimed, not without justification, that he now commanded the lake.[7] On Lake Erie, American sailors contrived to capture two vessels from the British (though one of them had to be destroyed) and, as on Ontario, converted others. The elements of a base, collected at Black Rock, were transferred to Erie. On both lakes, the Americans began to build formidable warships. The *Madison,* a twenty-four-gun corvette, larger than any British vessel on the Lakes, was launched at Sackets Harbor on 26 November, 1812; Chauncey reported with pride,

"She was built in the short time of forty-five days; and nine weeks ago the timber that she is composed of was growing in the forest."[8]

Ships, however, were not the worst menace to British power on the Lakes. The new American squadrons were commanded and manned by professional naval officers and seamen. Against these people the Canadian Provincial Marine was incapable of contending effectively, for its officers were little more than ferry captains, and most of them were unequal to leadership in action. That outspoken cleric, the Rector of York, called them "the greatest cowards that have ever lived."[9] With the United States Navy established on the Lakes, only the Royal Navy could make head against it; and it was going to have its hands full.

The greatest mistake of British military policy in North America in 1812-13 was the failure to maintain the original British naval control of the Lakes. It is not easy to fix the responsibility for this failure. In one of his last letters to Sir George Prevost, the Governor-in-Chief, Sir Isaac Brock wrote, "The enemy is making every exertion to gain a naval superiority on both lakes, which if they accomplish I do not see how we can retain the country."[10] Prevost himself in October and November 1812 urged the British government to send officers and men of the Royal Navy to take over the naval task on the Great Lakes.[11] The following spring this was done, but it was already almost too late. Part of the trouble was the fact that high policy was made in London, and it took a long time for letters to cross the Atlantic. Part, probably, was the slowness of the Royal Navy to appreciate the strategic importance of the Lakes, and its reluctance to tie up large naval resources in an inland theater. Part was certainly the natural American administrative advantages which have already been mentioned. Finally, if the Canadian Provincial Marine had been a real fighting navy, it would never have allowed the United States to establish naval bases and squadrons on the waters of Ontario and Erie.

The British, of course, were building ships, just as the Americans were, and these enabled them to continue the contest. During most of 1812 their control of the Lakes had been absolute, but 1813 was to witness a desperate and uncertain struggle for supremacy, which on Lake Erie would end in a decisive British defeat.

III

Late in the spring of 1813, Commodore Sir James Yeo, R.N., took command of the British naval forces on the Lakes, and personally assumed direct charge of affairs on Lake Ontario. While he confronted Chauncey, on Lake Erie Commander R. H. Barclay faced a new American leader, Master Commandant Oliver Hazard Perry. Before

Yeo reached the Lakes, Chauncey had carried out an operation which was to have a baneful effect on Barclay's fortunes.

The American raid on York (Toronto), late in April 1813, has been derided by military critics—not least by Admiral Mahan, who suggested quite soundly that Chauncey's proper objective was the main British naval base at Kingston, the capture of which would have destroyed the whole British position in Upper Canada. But although there is no evidence that Chauncey appreciated before the raid what its effect would be, it did the British far more harm than Mahan realized, and Chauncey's gleeful comment that it had inflicted on his enemy "a blow that he cannot recover" was not altogether without foundation. For one thing, the raid forced the British to burn the thirty-gun frigate *Sir Isaac Brock,* which was building at York, and which would have given them the safe command of Lake Ontario for that year. Still more important, however, was the fact that at York were the ordnance and naval stores intended to equip the British squadron on Lake Erie. These were either captured by the American raiders or destroyed by the British to save them from capture. This, combined with the subsequent interruption of the British communications by the capture of Fort George (at the mouth of the Niagara), meant that the armament and equipment for Barclay's flagship, the new corvette *Detroit,* never did reach Amherstburg.[12] The *Detroit* went into action on the fatal 10th of September armed with a curious assortment of guns from the ramparts of Fort Malden. The capture of York, indeed, had a good deal to do with the outcome of the Battle of Lake Erie.

I do not propose to describe the Battle of Lake Erie, for the story has often been told. But it is worth emphasizing that, in spite of Perry's dramatic and effective action at the crisis of the fight, it was more a logistical than a tactical victory. The Americans won because they had managed to create on Lake Erie a squadron stronger than their opponents', throwing a broadside of about twice the weight. Barclay's single chance of victory was lost when he relinquished his blockade of Erie long enough to let Perry get his two new brigs over the bar into the lake. Why Barclay did this has never been satisfactorily explained. Once the American squadron was complete on the lake, only gross tactical mismanagement by the Americans could allow the British to win in a stand-up fight. In fact, as everybody knows, there was serious mismanagement, and the British nearly did win; but Perry turned the tide by shifting his broad pendant from the *Lawrence* to the *Niagara* and bringing the latter ship into close action. By evening, after one of the bitterest small battles of the age of sail, the whole British squadron had been taken. From then until the end of the war the Americans controlled Lake Erie, with the results I have already mentioned. Such were the consequences of the American superiority in local resources and the exposed British line of communication.

IV

The disaster on Lake Erie undoubtedly administered a severe shock to the British political and naval authorities. Its effect appears in the strong measures taken in 1814 to avoid a similar defeat on Lake Ontario.

Operations on Ontario during 1813 had been inconclusive. Chauncey and Yeo both acted cautiously, building up their squadrons and refusing to engage except under conditions that made victory certain. There was more justification for this policy in Yeo's case than in Chauncey's. For the British, defeat on Lake Ontario would have been fatal; for the Americans it would have been merely embarrassing.

As a result the struggle for Lake Ontario in 1814 turned into "a shipbuilder's war."[13] The British made enormous efforts. Numbers of naval personnel and shipwrights appeared at Kingston. The movement of guns and other necessities for the new ships taxed the St. Lawrence transport system to the limit. The Admiralty, attaching new importance to the Lakes, made them a separate command; Yeo was made a commander-in-chief, an office almost unprecedented for an officer of such low rank.[14] The Americans on their side took parallel measures. There were no battles, for neither party would risk defeat; but the ships got bigger and bigger. Yeo's sixty-gun *Prince Regent* and forty-four-gun *Princess Charlotte* were countered by Chauncey's *Superior* of sixty-two and *Mohawk* of forty-two. The British government, to the disgust of its servants in Canada, sent ships from England in pieces, to be assembled at Kingston. A fifty-six-gun frigate was produced in this manner. Then Yeo sought to obtain definitive command of the lake by a great stroke; he built a tremendous three-decker, more powerful than Nelson's *Victory*—the *St. Lawrence,* which could carry up to one hundred and twelve guns. With this ship Yeo exercised undisputed control of Lake Ontario in the last weeks of the navigation season of 1814. But the only result was that the Americans began to build *two* three-deckers of one hundred and twenty guns, which if completed would have been the largest vessels in the world at that time. The British promptly laid down two more. None of these last four ships was ever launched, for the treaty of peace put an end to this extraordinary competition.[15] They remained on the stocks for years, monuments to the recognition by British and Americans alike of the enormous importance of the naval command of Lake Ontario.

I should say one word here of the naval situation on Lake Huron. Here the vital consideration for the British was the maintenance of communication with their distant garrison at Michilimackinac. Perry's victory cut the direct line of supply, but by one expedient and another Michilimackinac was maintained until the end of the war. Reinforcements were sent to it in the autumn of 1814 by the canoe route along the Ottawa and French Rivers and the north shore of Lake Huron.[16] More important was the overland portage from York via Lake Simcoe to the Nottawasaga River at the lower end of Georgian Bay, and thence by ship to Mackinac. This route was seriously threatened in August 1814 when the Americans destroyed in the Nottawasaga the one British vessel still navigating Lake Huron, the schooner *Nancy*. The *Nancy's* crew, however, survived the disaster and, resorting to boat attack, captured the two American schooners, *Tigress* and *Scorpion,* which had been left to maintain the blockade.[17] Communication with Mackinac by lake was thus ensured for the time being. When the war ended, the British were busy making preparations to regain the naval command of the upper lakes. During the winter of 1814-15 a road was laboriously built from Lake Simcoe to Penetanguishene, which had been selected as a base on Georgian Bay. Here preparations were made to build a frigate which, at first planned to carry twenty-four to twenty-six guns, soon grew to forty-four.[18] If the war had lasted another year, there would have been a resumption of large-scale naval competition and conflict on the upper lakes.

V

It is appropriate to conclude with a look at events on Lake Champlain. This lake was enormously important strategically because of its position on the ancient eastern invasion route across the border. The Hudson valley and the lake constituted a natural corridor through the highlands, which had always been utilized by armies crossing the border in either direction. It would have been better for the Americans, as we have seen, if they had made their main effort through this corridor. As it was, in 1814 the British, having been reinforced from Europe, mounted an invasion of New York state on this line. Sir George Prevost's fine army marched south, flanked on the water by a British naval squadron whose flagship still had ship carpenters on board working to complete her. In the bay of Plattsburg, a year and a day after Perry's victory on Lake Erie, this squadron fought the new American ships commanded by Captain Thomas Macdonough,

U.S.N., and was totally defeated. Prevost at once broke off the invasion and retired to Canada. He has been much criticized for goading the British naval commander, Downie, into premature action, and for failing to support him by attacking the American batteries on shore. But no competent critic, then or since, has ever denied that Prevost had no choice but to retreat once Downie's force had been destroyed. Offensive operations on the Lake Champlain line were possible only for a commander in control of the lake.

The greatest British military commander of that age has commented on the absolute necessity of naval command of the lakes. When the news of Prevost's misfortune reached England, the Duke of Wellington had completed his victorious campaign in the Peninsula and the south of France, and Napoleon had been sent to Elba. The British government now offered Wellington the command in America. The Duke's reply reflected both his strategic judgment and his rugged common sense. If the government wanted "conquests" in America, he said, what was needed was "not a general, nor general officers and troops," but superiority on the lakes:

Till that superiority is acquired, it is impossible, according to my notion, to maintain an army in such a situation as to keep the enemy out of the whole frontier, much less to make any conquest from the enemy, which, with those superior means, might, with reasonable hopes of success, be undertaken. . . . The question is, whether we can obtain this naval superiority on the lakes. If we cannot, I shall do you but little good in America; and I shall go there only to prove the truth of Prevost's defense, and to sign a peace which might as well be signed now.[19]

It was now clear that the pursuit of naval superiority was likely to be, in words used by Sir James Yeo a few months later, "an endless if not a futile undertaking."[20] Moreover, as the British government looked at the state of Europe, it realized that it might shortly have employment for Wellington more important than any he was likely to find in the American woods. It proceeded to take his advice, and made peace with the United States. It would seem that the same line of reasoning prevailed a couple of years later, when the British ministry decided to accept the American proposals for naval disarmament on the Lakes.[21]

NOTES

1. See the present writer's "An American Plan for a Canadian Campaign," *American Historical Review,* XLVI (January, 1941).

2. A. T. Mahan, *Sea Power in its Relations to the War of 1812,* 2 vols. (New York, 1905), I, 362.

3. I have discussed the question of communications and logistics in a documented article, "Another Look at the Battle of Lake Erie," *Canadian Historical Review,* XXXIX (March, 1958).

4. *Pittsburgh Directory for 1815* (Pittsburgh, 1815; republished, chiefly in facsimile, Pittsburgh, 1905). Cf. "Another Look at the Battle of Lake Erie," note 3, above.

5. *Documents relating to the Invasion of Canada and the Surrender of Detroit, 1812,* ed. E. A. Cruikshank (Ottawa, 1913), p. 188.

6. Mahan, I, 354.

7. For documentation, see C. P. Stacey, "Commodore Chauncey's Attack on Kingston Harbor, November 10, 1812," *Canadian Historical Review,* XXXII (June, 1951).

8. Mahan, I, 366.

9. "John Strachan to James McGill, Nov., 1812," *The John Strachan Letter Book: 1812-1834,* ed. G. W. Spragge (Toronto, 1946), pp. 27-28.

10. "Sir Isaac Brock, 11 Oct., 1812," in F. B. Tupper, *The Life and Correspondence of Major-General Sir Isaac Brock, K. B.,* 2nd ed. (London, 1847), p. 325.

11. "Another Look at the Battle of Lake Erie," note 3, above.

12. "Prevost to Bathurst, 20 July, 1813," Public Archives of Canada, Q, CXXII, 92-94.

13. This is the title of an article by C. Winton-Clare, *Mariner's Mirror,* July, 1943. See also E. A. Cruikshank, "The Contest for the Command of Lake Ontario in 1814," *Ontario Historical Society Papers and Records,* XXI (1924).

14. Mahan, II, 330.

15. See the present writer's "The Ships of the British Squadron on Lake Ontario, 1812-14," *Canadian Historical Review,* XXXIV (December, 1953). An excellent book which throws light on British as well as American ships is Howard I. Chapelle, *The History of the American Sailing Navy* (New York, 1949).

16. "Prevost to Bathurst, 8 Nov., 1814," Public Archives of Canada, Q, CXXVIII, pt. 2, 425-26.

17. Mahan, II, 324-26.

18. "Yeo to Croker, 14 Oct., 1814," Public Archives of Canada, M. 389.6, pp. 226-30; "to Prevost, 26 Nov., 1814," Q, CXXVIII, pt. 2, 497-98. Cf. Sir George Head, *Forest Scenes and Incidents in the Wilds of North America* (London, 1829).

19. Mahan, II, 430-31 (to Lord Liverpool, 9 Nov., 1814).

20. "Yeo to Melville, 30 May, 1815," Public Archives of Canada, M. 389.6, pp. 307-12.

21. C. P. Stacey, "The Myth of the Unguarded Frontier, 1815-1871," *American Historical Review,* LVI (October, 1950).

THE ROLE OF THE INDIAN IN THE WAR

Reginald Horsman

FOR THE INDIANS, as for the major contenders, the events of the period from 1812 to 1815 were inextricably bound up with the history of the previous half-century. During the War of 1812 the Indians made their last great effort to retain at least a portion of the land between the Ohio and the Mississippi Rivers. The struggle for this area had begun as early as the conspiracy of Pontiac in 1763. It had continued through Dunmore's War, the Revolution, and the American-Indian wars of the 1780's and 1790's. It had flared up again in the confederacy of Tecumseh after 1805, and in the War of 1812 the struggle passed from climax to anti-climax as the Indians fought, were vanquished, and lost all hope of further effective resistance.

In their struggle for the land of the Old Northwest the Indians had since 1775 leaned heavily upon British assistance. British motives were by no means altruistic. During the Revolution the British had used the Indians in an effort to quell the rebellious colonists. After the achievement of American independence, British assistance to the Indians was given primarily to prevent American expansion into the land of the Old Northwest. The British feared that such an advance would produce Indian war, menace the British fur trade, and even endanger the safety of Canada. There were ample reasons for such fears.[1]

The Indians likewise had their own motives for the aid they gave to the British. The Indians realized quite clearly that the Americans were pushing an agricultural frontier westward across the American continent, and that this agricultural frontier threatened their existence. Even in the Revolutionary period the Indians saw that the British could hold out the hope of a distant administration, encouragement of the fur trade, and the restriction of settlement. After independence the choice was even clearer, for the British encouraged the Indians to retain land which the British no longer owned, but over parts of which

60

they still traded. The British and the Indians were natural allies in this period, and the alliance was made firmer by the adhesion of leading Indian agents and traders to the British cause in the Revolution. The Johnsons and John Butler on the Niagara frontier, and Alexander McKee, Matthew Elliott, and the Girtys on the Detroit frontier all had the strongest ties to the Indians, and the Indian Department in Canada depended on these loyalists and their descendants until the end of the War of 1812.

Yet, though the British and the Indians were natural allies in the period from 1775 to 1815, this alliance had lost its early vigor by the time of the War of 1812. The Indians still realized that the British alliance was their only hope, but many tribes that had been fighting since the beginning of the Revolution were now wary of committing themselves unreservedly to the British cause. This hesitation stemmed partly from an increased respect for American power, but it was also the result of the vagaries of British policy in the preceding years. Those tribes that had fought in the Revolution and in the Indian wars of the 1780's and 1790's had twice been deserted by the British.

The first desertion occurred in 1783, when the United States achieved its independence by the Treaty of Paris. In this treaty the Indians were ignored, and the new American nation was given the land westward to the Mississippi. This included the land of those tribes which had fought, often successfully, on the British side in the Revolution; it also included the land of tribes that hardly knew that there had been a Revolution. A second betrayal had come in 1794. From 1783 to 1794 the Indians renewed a bitter warfare against the ill-united, ill-armed, and impoverished American government. Though the British did not openly encourage the Indians to attack the American frontier, they did encourage the Indians to resist the American demands for land, and argued that the British had ceded only territorial sovereignty—not the right to the soil—in 1783. American demands, Indian intransigence, and British encouragement brought all-out war northwest of the Ohio by the end of the 1780's; after 1790 the British based on Detroit gave liberally of supplies and encouragement to the Indians of the Northwest. This phase of the struggle for the Old Northwest came to an end when General Anthony Wayne defeated the Indians at the battle of Fallen Timbers in 1794, and secured much of what is now eastern and southern Ohio in the following year at the Treaty of Greenville. The manner of this victory gave yet another blow to Indian belief in the good faith of the British in Canada. Though British agents had encouraged the Indians to stand firm, and had liberally issued supplies, the Indians were disgusted at the last instant by the failure of the British to provide more than token military aid. Though a hundred militia from Detroit fought with the Indians at Fallen Timbers, the British Fort Miami barred its gates to the Indians retreating before Wayne's forces. This was long remembered, and was to help to make the Indians far more cautious allies of the British in the War of 1812.[2]

In spite of Indian disaffection in 1783 and 1794, they were again driven into the arms of the British in the following years. After 1794 American settlers moved rapidly down and across the Ohio, and poured into the area of the Greenville cession. Though the Greenville line was supposed to represent a "permanent" boundary, the Americans were by 1802 pressing the Indians for further cessions. In the years between 1802 and 1809 Governor William Henry Harrison of Indiana Territory pressed the Indians into ceding large areas of what are now Indiana and Illinois. Inevitably this produced further difficulties with the Indians. In 1805 Indian discontent focused on Greenville, Ohio, where a Shawnee prophet arose to preach an Indian religious revival, and urged the elimination of white influence. The religious movement of the Prophet soon became a political movement under the leadership of his talented brother, Tecumseh. Tecumseh was to be the most notable of the Indian leaders until his death in the War of 1812. Unfortunately, recent authors have tended to make him less a man than a myth. They have given him a colorful younger life, complete with a love affair with a beautiful white girl, and have made him in his mature years into an Indian Alexander. There is no need to exaggerate Tecumseh's merits. He was indeed a talented leader who made a determined attempt to unite the Indians in common resistance to the American settlers. Those who met him both before and during the war almost unanimously agreed on his integrity and his powers of leadership. There seems good reason to doubt, however, that his confederacy was ever the massive, tight-knit affair that it is often made out to be.[3]

From 1795 to 1807 the British had neglected the Indians of the Old Northwest, assuming that they would not again be needed to aid the British in a struggle against the Americans. This attitude changed in 1807 when events at sea once again threatened to bring war between England and the United States. After the *Chesapeake* affair in June 1807, it seemed likely that the United States would declare war on England and invade Canada. From 1807 to 1812 the British in Canada attempted to avert this threat by securing Indian aid for any future defense of Canada. The Indian discontent which had resulted in the rise of Tecumseh made this possible, but the memory of 1783 and 1794 made the Indians more cautious allies than they had been in earlier struggles.

The years from 1775 to 1812 had brought considerable changes along the border of Canada and the United States. In the east the Six Nations no longer represented the force of former days. The warriors who had brought such terror along the Mohawk and the Wyoming were now merely an island in a sea of American settlement. After the Revolution some of them had followed their great chief Joseph Brant to the Grand River region of Canada, others had remained on restricted lands within the United States. The Six Nations could yet be of use to the British along the Niagara frontier, but they were no longer the power of former days.

There had also been remarkable changes beyond the Ohio. At the beginning of the Revolution there had been no American settlement northwest of the Ohio (though the first pioneers were pushing into Kentucky). By 1810 Ohio had nearly a quarter of a million inhabitants, and settlers were pushing into Indiana and Illinois. Detroit was no longer the British post dominating the western country, for in 1796 it had been handed over to the Americans. The British now based their operations on the post of Malden, and the adjoining village of Amherstburg, some seventeen miles below Detroit on the Canadian side of the river. From Amherstburg Britain sought to influence the Indians of the Old Northwest in the years prior to 1812. Shawnees, Wyandots, Delawares, Miamis, Ottawas, Chippewas, Potawatomis, and many others came into Amherstburg to receive supplies and encouragement from the British Superintendent Elliott.

The influence of Amherstburg extended even to the area west of Lake Michigan. Though that vast area was nominally American, the influence of the British fur traders was paramount until the close of the War of 1812. By the beginning of the war Robert Dickson, the most prominent British fur trader on the Upper Mississippi, had some two hundred and fifty or three hundred Indians ready to proceed to the British post on St. Joseph Island, east of Mackinac, and he had prepared many other potential allies. Moreover, in January, 1812, the powerful North West and South West fur companies promised that they would help in military actions west of Lake Michigan, and that they would use their influence to secure the assistance of the Indians. In this region west of Lake Michigan England was in her strongest position with the Indians, for they had been comparatively untouched by the events of the 1775-95 period.

The sharp deterioration in American-Indian relations brought an outbreak of hostilities in the Old Northwest even before England and the United States were at war. In November, 1811, at the battle of Tippecanoe in Indiana Territory, Governor William Henry Harrison clashed with forces of Tecumseh. Harrison dispersed Tecumseh's force while Tecumseh was away among the southern Indians, and from that time until the actual outbreak of war between England and the United States there were sporadic outbreaks of Indian hostility along the frontiers of the Old Northwest. The Indians were fighting because they had no other real choice before the advance of the American frontier. There is no doubt that by the beginning of the War of 1812 the great majority of the Indians on the frontiers of Upper Canada were hostile to the Americans and were potential British allies. But there was still doubt as to the extent to which the Indians would throw themselves unreservedly into the British cause. Great Britain would have to show by effective aggressive action on the United States-Canadian border—against Detroit or Michilimackinac—that she intended to fight this war in earnest, and that she would supply regular troops to aid her Indian auxiliaries.[4]

The American declaration of war against Great Britain took place on June 18, 1812, and within one month the British had used the Indians to win a notable victory in the region west of Lake Michigan. The officer in command at the British post of St. Joseph, Captain Charles Roberts, received news of the declaration of war on July 8. He acted with commendable swiftness, and on July 16 led an expedition to assault the American post on Mackinac Island. Though he had only a small regular garrison, he was able to enlist the aid of local Canadians (many of them employed by the North West Company) and of the Indians. This provided him with a total force of between seven and eight hundred, of which half were Indian. Over one hundred and forty of these were Sioux, Winnebago, and Menominee brought in by Robert Dickson, and there were also some three hundred Chippewa and Ottawa raised by John Askin, Jr., who was the British storekeeper at St. Joseph. This force greatly outnumbered the Americans available at Michilimackinac, and on July 17 that vital American post surrendered without resistance. This was a great blow to the American cause, not only west of Lake Michigan but throughout the whole Northwest. It gave the British a hold on the region west of Lake Michigan which they did not relinquish until the peace of Ghent.[5]

The Indians of this area now flocked to the aid of the British with the enthusiasm of the Six Nations in the Revolution or the Ohio and Indiana Indians in the late 1780's and early '90's. In the middle of August another American post—Fort Dearborn at the mouth of the Chicago River—fell before the aroused warriors. The garrison was overwhelmed as it attempted to retreat southward to Fort Wayne. This left only one American fort, Fort Madison on the Mississippi, in the region west of Lake Michigan. That too suffered an attack at the beginning of September, 1812, but the Winnebago failed to overwhelm the garrison. This could hardly lighten American gloom, for the other two main settlements in the area, Green Bay and Prairie du Chien, were also in the hands of British sympathizers, and Fort Madison itself was abandoned a year later in November, 1813.[6]

American efforts to regain the intiative in this distant theater of the war proved unsuccessful. For a time in the summer of 1814 an American force did occupy Prairie du Chien and erect Fort Shelby, but a British force (composed mainly of Indians) came from Mackinac and Green Bay and recaptured that vital spot. Another American attempt to take Prairie du Chien was made in September, but the expedition under Major Zachary Taylor was repulsed by British artillery and a large force of Indians before it even reached the object of its mission.[7] British control over the Indians ensured their success in the region west of Lake Michigan throughout the War of 1812.

The capture of Michilimackinac and the assertion of British strength west of Lake Michigan had an effect which extended far beyond its immediate area. All along the American-Canadian border, tribes were inspired by that distant event, and from a more practical point of view the extent of British control beyond Mackinac freed tribes to join the British in other areas of fighting—in particular along the Detroit frontier.

The United States began the War of 1812 with the avowed object of invading and conquering Canada. The general plan of conquest called for blows along the Hudson Valley and Lake Champlain to Montreal, across the Niagara peninsula, and across the Detroit River into Upper Canada. For utmost effectiveness these blows should have been synchronized, and the greatest weight should have been given to the easternmost attack. A successful attack on Montreal would have reduced the British possessions in the West to impotence. Politically, however, this plan of attack proved impossible. The western regions had the greatest enthusiasm for the war and were prepared to provide men, but they were not enthusiastic for an eastern war. The westerners wanted to attack the British post of Fort Malden, conquer Upper Canada, and remove the threat of Indian attack from the area northwest of the Ohio.[8]

This preoccupation with the danger of Indian attack from the Amherstburg region was to produce dissipation of American effort in the first year of the war. Once the decision to attack in the West was made, it was essential to win a quick victory to allow concentration on eastern areas of the war. It was in preventing this quick victory that the Indians played their most important role in the War of 1812. They were decisive in preventing a quick victory at a time when it would not only have provided a great boost to American morale but would also have allowed concentration on the vital areas further east.

As the war began General William Hull was advancing northward out of Ohio to Detroit. Hull, who reached Detroit on July 5, had at his disposal over two thousand men. At Malden Britain had some three hundred regulars, and could probably count on some eight hundred militia. There was not the slightest doubt that the attitude of the Indians was to be of the utmost importance in deciding the fate of the American campaign. Hull realized this, and made every effort to persuade the Indians to stay neutral in the coming struggle. His efforts for the most part resulted in failure. Though some of the Indians of Ohio and Indiana maintained neutrality, and though a few even fought on the American side, a decisive number joined the British. By the beginning of July, Tecumseh and Elliott, the British superintendent at Amherstburg, had gathered some three or four hundred warriors. These became of vital importance on July 12, when the American force at last crossed the Detroit River and occupied Sandwich. Their importance was increased by the readiness with which many of the Canadian militia responded to Hull's proclamation promising protection for those who remained at home. Fort Malden and Amherstburg now appeared in imminent danger of falling into American hands.[9]

Hull's failure to achieve a victory has often been ascribed to his own shortcomings, but in truth there were certain definite weaknesses in his position. As the Americans did not have naval control of Lake Erie, Hull had to depend for his supplies and reinforcements on the tenuous and difficult land route from Detroit into Ohio. This American line of supply was highly vulnerable to Indian attack, particularly in the stretch that ran along the west bank of the Detroit River. By the beginning of August there seemed a definite threat that this supply line would be severed. On August 5 Tecumseh and a small party of warriors ambushed one hundred and fifty Ohio militiamen who were coming out of Detroit to carry mail, and to bring supplies from the River Raisin. This ambush was a complete success, and the militiamen fled in terror. Four days later another ambush, this time at Monguagon between Brownstown and Detroit, was less successful. In this ambush the Indians were joined by British regulars. The British force attacked an American contingent of some six hundred men who had been sent from Detroit to clear the line of communication. On this occasion it was the British and Indians who were forced to retreat, but it was quite clear to Hull that his line of supply was at best a tenuous one, and that he faced the danger of constant Indian harassment in his rear. This fear was compounded early in August by the news of the fall of Fort Michilimackinac. Hull now expected many Indians from that region to join the British forces. Indians were in fact to come from that region, but not in the numbers that Hull expected, nor in time to be of interest to him in his campaign.[10]

Faced by an Indian threat to his line of communications, and dreading the arrival of a horde of Indians from the west, Hull decided to recross the Detroit River and take refuge in Detroit rather than risk an attack on Fort Malden. Initiative passed to the British and the Indians, and their cause was immediately strengthened. The Indian force increased to some six hundred warriors, and the British force gained a vigorous commander and a reinforcement of over three hundred men when Major-General Isaac Brock arrived on the night of August 13. Brock acted quickly. During the night of August 15-16 some six hundred Indians under the command of Elliott and Tecumseh crossed the Detroit River to attack Detroit. The British force followed on the next day. Hull, fearful and indecisive, thought of his isolation, of the non-combatants under his care, and of Brock's warning that should he be forced to take Detroit by storm he could not guarantee controlling the Indians. Hull decided to surrender without resistance.[11]

It is difficult to exaggerate the importance of the Indians in the entire Hull fiasco. Their presence, and his fear of further Indian reinforcements, had been decisive in his retreat across the Detroit River, and their presence in the attacking British force had been decisive in his surrender without a fight. The surrender of Detroit was a crushing blow to the Americans. They had depended upon Hull and his enthusiastic westerners to begin with a flourish the task of conquering Canada. American morale was weakened, as was the war effort on other fronts, and the task of invasion had been made far more difficult. Moreover, the surrender of Detroit, when added to the surrender of Michilimackinac and the massacre at Fort Dearborn, was enough to bring several hundred Indians of the Six Nations into the British camp on the Niagara frontier. The surrender also allowed Brock to rush east and take charge of the British defenses in that same region. Though he was to die at the battle of Queenston Heights in October, that battle was to result in yet another successful repulse of the American forces, with warriors of the Six Nations fighting alongside the British troops.[12]

Though the Indians had proved of great importance in the first few months of the war, they were to meet with considerable criticism in the following year, particularly when the British forces attempted offensive operations in the Northwest. There was marked friction between the regular army officers and the Indians, and between the regular officers and the members of the British Indian Department. The regular officers disliked the independent nature of the Indians; it was too much like associating with irregular guerilla bands. This difficulty of cooperation was accentuated by the role of the British Indian Department, which tended to take the Indian side in nearly every argument. Since the Revolution the British Indian Department at Detroit had been composed of loyalists who had fled from western Pennsylvania. These men had no love for the Americans, and they had spent a lifetime among the Indians. Matthew Elliott, who was superintendent at Amherstburg during the war, had two half-Indian sons fighting for the British in the conflict (one was killed early in the war), and he had great sympathy for the Indian point of view.

There is no doubt that the Indians were not amenable to the type of discipline preferred by the regular officers. In spite of the influence of Tecumseh, they tended to ignore the strategy of the conflict, and to think of quick victories which produced plunder and scalps. Such a victory was usually followed by a general dispersal of the Indians to their villages for a celebration. The Indians also showed a marked preference for certain types of warfare. They disliked formal fighting in orderly ranks, and preferred to suffer as few losses as possible; losses usually meant retreat and dispersal rather than increased stubbornness. The Indians preferred to attack from ambush, and were most reluctant to attack in the open against entrenched fortifications. Indian forces were notoriously weak in taking the flimsiest fortifications unless accompanied by British artillery. To the regular officers the Indians were an unreliable force which could not be depended upon to follow the strategy laid down by the British, and which posed great problems of supply.

The manner in which the Indians waged war was also a severe embarrassment to the British regulars; they were often shocked by the killing and torturing of prisoners and non-combatants. In spite of myths to the contrary most British soldiers and civil officials greatly regretted Indian atrocities and tried to prevent them. It was of course a price that had to be paid for enlisting Indian support, but efforts were made to restrain Indian excesses. The members of the Indian Department tended to be somewhat more callous, primarily because they were often men who had spent a lifetime among the Indians, married them, fought with them, and sometimes fought like them. They were accustomed to the Indian way of life, and they were no more shocked by the burning of a prisoner than a regular army officer was shocked by the flogging to death of a soldier for a military offense.

The difficulties which could beset British-Indian relations were well illustrated by the unsuccessful expedition led by Major Adam Muir against Fort Wayne in September 1812. After the American loss of Mackinac, Detroit, and Fort Dearborn, exposed Fort Wayne was in a most precarious position, and at the beginning of September 1812 news reached Amherstburg that it was besieged by the Indians. Procter wanted to send Elliott to prevent the Indians from committing excesses, but as Elliott was ill he merely sent messages asking for moderation. When, shortly after, the Indians requested aid, Procter sent some three hundred and fifty troops and eight hundred Indians to their assistance. Among the Indians were some two hundred who had recently arrived from Mackinac. The expedition was a failure, for it never reached Fort Wayne. After travelling to within about forty miles of the fort, the British force encountered a larger American force advancing northward under the command of Brigadier General James Winchester. Considerable confusion ensued as the Indians, who had thought they were going to overwhelm a small American fort after it had been shattered by British guns, showed reluctance to meet a superior American force. They could not agree on the correct place to make a stand, and many drifted off. By the time a part of the Indian force decided that it would fight, Muir himself had resolved that it would now be suicidal and ordered a retreat. Muir reported adversely on the conduct of the Indians in this affair, and the British commander at Malden, Colonel Henry Procter, blamed the Indian Department for the lack of effective Indian assistance. This produced increased tension between Procter and Superintendent Elliott.[13] Although Procter attacked the Indians and the Indian Department, he could hardly have carried on without them. They had proved their worth in the summer of 1812, and were to prove it again early in 1813.

The American army in the Northwest was quite naturally under considerable pressure to redeem the tragic loss of Detroit, and to carry the war to Fort Malden and Upper Canada. In command of the American armies in this region was William Henry Harrison; after failing to organize an effective attack in the fall of 1812, Harrison decided in favor of a risky winter attack against Fort Malden. The attack never took place, for before it really began General Winchester committed a blunder which ended American hopes.

In January, 1813, the French at Frenchtown (on the River Raisin below Detroit) requested the Americans to come to their relief, and pointed out that there were a good many supplies which could readily be taken by the Americans. The Frenchmen at the River Raisin had long disliked the British in Canada. Winchester heeded this request, and moved his army from the rapids of the Maumee to Frenchtown. Part of his force easily defeated the small garrison. Winchester had little time to enjoy his victory, for Procter, acting with untypical swiftness, immediately led a British force of some six hundred men, with more than that number of Indians, across the frozen Detroit River to attack the American position. Not all of the American force was within the pickets of the town, and it was the section outside that broke when it was flanked by the Indians. Winchester himself was captured, and though there was still considerable American resistance within the town he decided to surrender the American force as he feared a general Indian massacre if the battle continued. As at Detroit the presence of the Indian warriors was an essential ingredient in the British victory, but this time the surrender did not prevent a massacre. On the night of the victory the Indians moved in among the American wounded, and slaughtered some thirty of them. The British commander, Procter, and Superintendent Elliott must share the blame, for they had quickly withdrawn to Amherstburg after the engagement, leaving insufficient protection for the American prisoners. It seems likely that the great dissension between Procter and the Indian Department had made the discussion of policy increasingly difficult, and had contributed to the tragic ending of the battle.[14]

The macabre episode greatly increased American bitterness against both the Indians and the British. The Indians had again proved their ability both to achieve victories and at the same time to embarrass their allies. Events in the spring of 1813 followed a similar pattern. Procter failed to follow up his victory at the River Raisin with prompt action, and it was not until the end of April that he led a British force along the Maumee River into American territory. His object was the American Fort Meigs which had been constructed during the winter at the rapids of the Maumee. Procter's force consisted of nearly one thousand white troops and twelve hundred Indians under Elliott and Tecumseh. The British hoped to take the fort by siege, but were doomed to disappointment. The British artillery could not breach the defenses, and the Indians were of little value with the Americans safely established in their recently constructed fortifications.

The course of the siege of Fort Meigs apparently turned decisively in favor of the Americans when news arrived that Brigadier General

Green Clay had reached the Glaize with a force of twelve hundred Kentuckians. Harrison decided to relieve British pressure on the fort, and ordered some eight hundred men from Clay's force to attack the British batteries opposite Fort Meigs on the other side of the river. They were to destroy what they could, spike the guns, and retreat. Though the maneuver was at first successful, the Americans failed to retreat in time, were outflanked by the Indians under Tecumseh, and were completely routed when British troops drove into their center. The Indians, as at the River Raisin, had proved their value when facing American troops in the open, but once again a massacre followed the battle. After the American prisoners were removed to the ruins of the old British Fort Miami, the Indians moved in among them and slaughtered forty or more. Procter had again failed to provide for the safety of his prisoners, and on this occasion it was Tecumseh (who had not been present at the River Raisin) who rode into the fort and stopped the massacre.[15]

The British had won a notable victory over the American force, but had not carried out the object of their mission—the reduction of Fort Meigs. The task now became practically impossible, for after the victory the Indians dispersed with their prisoners and booty, and the militia also wanted to return home. The British were finding it as difficult as the Americans to take the offensive on the Detroit front, and their position became increasingly precarious during the summer of 1813. Amherstburg was at the end of a long British line of communications, and since the beginning of the war there had been constant difficulty in supplying the Indians of the region. By the summer of 1813 the lack of provisions seemed likely to produce a dispersion of the Indians, particularly as the Indians were disgusted by the lack of a recent victory. To relieve the pressure on provisions, and in the hope of snatching this victory, Procter decided once again to take the offensive.

In July, 1813, Procter once again led a British army against Fort Meigs. He took with him several hundred British troops and militia and about one thousand Indians; many of these Indians had come from the region west of Lake Michigan to join in the campaigns on the Detroit frontier. The attack on Fort Meigs was a failure. The fort was too well defended, and the only British hope was an Indian plan to lure the Americans from the fort by a feigned attack on an imaginary American relieving force. The Americans were not deceived, and Procter withdrew his force from Fort Meigs, leading it down the Maumee, along Lake Erie, and up the Sandusky to the small American post of Fort Stephenson. Though this fort was garrisoned by less than two hundred American troops, the British attack again was a failure.

Procter hoped that the garrison of Fort Stephenson would surrender without a struggle, and in negotiations with the American commander, Major George Croghan, he used the old argument that if the fort were taken by storm the Indians could not be restrained. This did not work, and a joint British and Indian attack was agreed upon. This failed. The Indians had been reluctant to take part in the attack, and, when the time came for them to begin their part of the assault, they withdrew before getting into the range of the guns of the fort. The Indians looked upon the reduction of forts as a task for the guns of their allies, and they had no intention of being slaughtered in a futile attack. Many left even before the assault took place, and after it there was a further dispersal of the Indian force. Procter now withdrew to Fort Malden. The campaign against Fort Meigs and Fort Stephenson had been a singularly undistinguished one, and had only increased the distrust between the British regulars and the Indians. Procter tried to blame the failure of the whole campaign on the weaknesses of the Indians and of the Indian Department, but the British Commander-in-Chief, Sir George Prevost, indicated that he thought little of Procter's judgment.[16]

The first year of the war had brought the British no real success in their offensive operations on the Detroit frontier, but they might well be satisfied at their over-all record. At the beginning of the war the United States had confidently expected to overwhelm Fort Malden and conquer Upper Canada. It had failed in this object, had lost Detroit, and had suffered other reverses at the River Raisin and at the first siege of Fort Meigs. Though Procter had been energetic in his criticism of the Indians and the Indian Department, they had played an essential part in all of the British victories. The Indians for their part were critical of British operations on the Detroit frontier, of the shortage of provisions, and of the failure of British artillery to overwhelm American fortifications. Their criticism of British policy reached a peak in the fall of 1813, when the whole tide of the war on the Detroit frontier was changed by Commander Oliver H. Perry's victory over the British fleet on Lake Erie at the battle of Put-in-Bay. At long last the United States had severed the British line of supply to Fort Malden. This was far more effective in overcoming British resistance than all the maneuverings of American armies along the Maumee.

The United States now controlled Lake Erie, and Procter's position at Amherstburg was untenable. Yet, if he could win a victory before retiring, he could considerably improve his position, and also help to retain the allegiance of the Indians. By this time there were several thousand Indians at Amherstburg, and though this was a considerable strain on British supplies, it gave the British an excellent chance of defeating the American army under General Harrison which was advancing to attack Fort Malden after Commander Perry's victory. Tecumseh and his Indians were ardently in favor of defending Fort Malden. They could not understand why a naval victory should necessitate a retreat from established positions, and Tecumseh told Procter in council that "We must compare our father's conduct to a fat animal that carries its tail upon its back, but when affrighted, it drops between its legs and runs off." But, in spite of Tecumseh's protestations and the opinion of the Indian Department, Procter determined on retreat. He took his force northward along the east bank of the Detroit River, turned east along the southern shore of Lake St. Clair, and retreated along the Thames River. As he retreated, his large Indian force began to disintegrate.[17]

Procter finally made his stand at Moraviantown on the Thames. Even here there was disagreement. Tecumseh and Superintendent Elliott thought Procter had taken up the wrong position. The Indian force had been sadly reduced, and the British troops had little faith in Procter. The result was disaster for the British. The Americans attacked on October 5, and the British troops, their morale shattered by Procter's retreat, broke in confusion. Tecumseh and his Indians fought desperately. Tecumseh was killed, and a total of some thirty-three Indians were left dead on the field; others undoubtedly were carried away. The British lost only twelve men, but six hundred were taken prisoner. These figures demonstrated the full loss of faith in Procter.[18]

The battle of the Thames (or Moraviantown as it is called in Canada) was the decisive battle of the war on the Detroit frontier, and the decisive battle for the Indians of the whole region. It meant more to them than the loss of a single battle, for this was also their last great battle in defense of the Old Northwest. Tecumseh was dead, and he joined a host of warriors who had fought since before the Revolution to save the land between the Ohio and the Mississippi. The main struggle was now over. There were to be no more great battles for the Old Northwest.

The War of 1812 continued, and the Americans now had complete control of the Detroit region. The Indians of the area either had to acquiesce in American control, or follow Procter and his retreating army eastward to the Niagara frontier. There the war was still bitterly fought, but the Detroit front was to remain quiet for the remainder of the conflict.

In the Niagara region the western Indians who had followed Superintendent Elliott continued to aid the British. To this point the main brunt of Indian resistance in this area had been borne by the Six Nations. Though at first they had been reluctant to join the British cause, the victories of Mackinac and Detroit in the summer of 1812 had won over several hundred of the old Revolutionary allies. They had fought on the British side at the battle of Queenston Heights, and a number stayed with the British even after the Americans had captured

Fort George (across the Niagara River from Fort Niagara) in May 1813, and the British had retreated to the head of Lake Ontario. There they were joined by additional Indian reinforcements from Lower Canada, and the Indian warriors succeeded in making the captured Fort George a most dangerous American outpost. Though the Indians of Lower Canada returned home, the British at the head of the lake were then reinforced by Matthew Elliott and his western Indians. These served effectively in the winter campaigns of 1813-14, in which the British retook Fort George (in December 1813) and then made raids across the Niagara River against Lewiston, Black Rock, and Buffalo. The attack on Lewiston was a violent one, and it brought renewed American complaints of Indian atrocities. A hundred or so western Indians continued to serve with the British and the Six Nations on the Niagara frontier until the American victory at the battle of Chippewa in July 1814. After that there was no significant Indian participation on the Niagara frontier.[19]

An effort to revive Indian hostility in the Detroit region failed in March 1814, when the western Indians who had accompanied the British to Lake Ontario refused to take arms and ammunition to their western brothers unless British regulars also returned to the Detroit frontier. The Indians feared that the smuggling in of arms and ammunition would only serve to bring stern American retaliation against the Indians in the American-occupied areas.[20]

Indian aid to the British, which had reached such notable proportions along the United States-Canadian border at the beginning of the War of 1812, was by the summer of 1814 for the most part confined to the area west of Lake Michigan. Indian assistance had for a time ranged from the Mississippi in the west to the St. Lawrence in the east. There was never, however, a total allegiance of the Indians to the British cause. Many, particularly in the eastern theaters of the war, remained neutral; a few even fought on the side of the Americans. Yet, though Indian support was not consistent, it provided a vital ingredient in the British military operations. West of Lake Michigan

Indian support was decisive in holding the area for the British until the very end of the war. On the Detroit front Indian support was the key element in blocking the first enthusiastic American offensive against Canada, and it dealt a stunning blow to American morale. In spite of the complaints of the military, it seems hardly possible that they could have occupied the Americans and won victories for a whole year in the Detroit region without Indian support. The Indians outnumbered the British troops at most of the engagements in this theater of war. and played a decisive part in the victories at Detroit, on the River Raisin, and in the first siege of Fort Meigs. They also performed most creditably at the British defeat at the battle of the Thames. For all the disadvantages of having irregular Indian support, the British could not have acted effectively without them. The role of the Indian was less important in the disillusioned regions farther to the east, but even in Lower Canada some joined the British forces.

For all this, there is no doubt that there is a danger of making too much of Indian effectiveness in the War of 1812. Their importance really stemmed from the inadequacy of the American attack. If the United States had prepared for and mounted an effective attack on the British province, it could have negated the value of Indian support for the British. In essence, the United States failed to take Canada not because of Indian resistance but because of inadequate preparations, poor planning, and inefficient leadership. Congress provided no real army, and an inadequate navy. Though the possibility of war had been discussed for several years, there were still fewer than ten thousand American regular troops when it began, and it was still uncertain whether the militia would cross the Canadian border and fight on foreign soil. The War Hawks and their allies showed for the most part a disastrous lack of interest in or positive aversion to the development of American naval power. They hoped and expected to march into Canada, but failed to take control of the vital St. Lawrence-Great Lakes waterway. If the United States had quickly seized naval control of the Lakes, the disasters and embarrassments of the western campaigns would not have occurred; Indian supplies would have been cut off, and the British regulars isolated. If this naval victory could have been followed by a firm, well-led action along the Hudson Valley-Lake Champlain route against Montreal, the Indians would have been only an irritant, not a decisive element. But as it was, American politics and the sectional nature of the support for the war overemphasized the western operations, and the American attack on Canada unfolded in a desultory manner from the west. Even so the invasion might have succeeded, given the weakness of the British regular forces in Canada, but the very inefficiency of the American offensive allowed the Indians to play a significant part in the British defense. The Indians helped to save Canada for Great Britain, but they lost the Old Northwest.

NOTES

1. Alfred L. Burt, *The United States, Great Britain, and British North America from the Revolution to the Establishment of Peace after the War of 1812* (New Haven, 1940), has the best discussion of the motives behind British retention of the Northwest posts, and assistance to the Indians.

2. For British aid to the Indians prior to 1795 see Randolph C. Downes, *Council Fires on the Upper Ohio: A Narrative of Indian Affairs in the Upper Ohio Valley until 1795* (Pittsburgh, 1940), and Reginald Horsman, "The British Indian Department and the Abortive Treaty of Lower Sandusky, 1793," *Ohio Historical Quarterly*, LXX (July, 1961), 189-213.

3. The standard modern account of Tecumseh is Glenn Tucker, *Tecumseh: Vision of Glory* (Indianapolis, 1956). It is a highly colored biography, and its main features are followed in the chapter on Tecumseh in Alvin R. Josephy, Jr., *The Patriot Chiefs: A Chronicle of American Indian Leadership* (New York, 1961). There is still need for a scholarly biography of Tecumseh.

4. British Indian policy in the pre-1812 war period is discussed in Reginald Horsman, "British Indian Policy in the Northwest, 1807-1812," *Mississippi Valley Historical Review*, XLV (June, 1958), 51-66.

5. For the events leading to the capture of Fort Michilimackinac see Alec R. Gilpin, *The War of 1812 in the Old Northwest* (East Lansing, Mich., 1958), pp. 88-93; see also Joseph and Estelle Bayliss, *Historic St. Joseph Island* (Cedar Rapids, Ia., 1938), pp. 55-64.

6. For these events west of Lake Michigan see Louise P. Kellogg, *The British Régime in Wisconsin and the Northwest* (Madison, Wis., 1935), pp. 285-97, 307-08.

7. *Ibid.*, pp. 313-25; Peter L. Scanlan, *Prairie du Chien: French, British, American* (Menasha, Wis., 1937), pp. 117-21; Bayliss, *Historic St. Joseph Island*, pp. 188-204.

8. A general account of the War of 1812 can be found in Henry Adams, *History of the United States*, 9 vols. (New York, 1889-91), Vols. VI, VII, and VIII. See also Francis F. Beirne, *The War of 1812* (New York, 1949), and Sir Charles P. Lucas, *The Canadian War of 1812* (Oxford, 1906). A recent account of the war in the Detroit region is Gilpin, *The War of 1812 in the Old Northwest*.

9. See Gilpin, *War of 1812*, pp. 29-83; "J. B. George to Isaac Brock, July 8, 10, 1812," "Matthew Elliott to William Claus, July 15, 1812," Public Archives of Canada (Ottawa), Series C. Military, RG 8, C 676, pp. 134-43, 180-82.

10. See *Richardson's War of 1812*, ed. Alexander C. Casselman (Toronto, 1902), pp. 26-36; *War on the Detroit: The Chronicles of Thomas Verchères de Boucherville, and The Capitulation by an Ohio Volunteer*, ed. Milo M. Quaife (Chicago, 1940), pp. 88-103; Milo

M. Quaife, "The Story of Brownstown," *Burton Historical Collection Leaflet*, IV, No. 5 (May, 1926), 65-80.

11. Gilpin, *War of 1812*, pp. 98-117; "Charles Askin's Journal of the Detroit Campaign," in *The John Askin Papers*, ed. Milo M. Quaife, 2 vols. (Detroit, 1928-31), II, 715-21; *Richardson's War of 1812*, ed. Casselman, pp. 49-79; "Brock to Sir George Prevost, August 17, 1812," Public Archives of Canada, Series C. Military, C 688-A, pp. 183-91; Ferdinand B. Tupper, *Life and Correspondence of Major General Sir Isaac Brock* (London, 1847), pp. 247-48.

12. There is a discussion of the attitude of the Six Nations in George F. G. Stanley, "The Indians in the War of 1812," *Canadian Historical Review*, XXXI (June, 1950), 155-56.

13. For the Muir expedition and tension between Procter and Elliott see "Procter to Brock, September 9, 1812," *Michigan Pioneer and Historical Collections*, 40 vols. (Lansing, Mich., 1877-1929), XV, 145; "Charles Askin's Journal," *Askin Papers*, ed. Quaife, II, 728-29, *Richardson's War of 1812*, ed. Casselman, pp. 93-103; "Muir to Procter, September 26, 30, 1812,' "Procter to Brock, October 3, 1812," "Procter to Sheaffe, October 30, 1812," "Dewar to McDonnell, October 19, 1812," Public Archives of Canada, Series C. Military, C 677, pp. 97-99, 102-12, 163-65, 136-39.

14. Adams, *History of the United States*, VII, 72-98; Gilpin, *War of 1812*, pp. 144-58, 163-71; *Richardson's War of 1812*, ed. Casselman, pp. 132-47.

15. The siege of Fort Meigs can be followed in *Richardson's War of 1812*, ed. Casselman, pp. 148-76; Gilpin, *War of 1812*, pp. 173-92; Adams, *History of the United States*, 103-08. For events at the massacre see Horace S. Knapp, *History of the Maumee Valley* (Toledo, O., 1877), p. 172, and *Draper Manuscripts*, 12YY63-64, State Historical Society, Madison, Wisconsin.

16. *Richardson's War of 1812*, ed. Casselman, pp. 177-88; "A. Battersby to Colonel Baynes, July 31, 1813," Public Archives of Canada, Series C. Military, C 679, pp. 517-20; Gilpin, *War of 1812*, pp. 202-08; Journal of Joseph H. Larwill, *Larwill Papers*, Burton Historical Collection, Detroit Public Library.

17. "Elliott to Claus, October 24, 1813," *Claus Papers*, MG 19, Series F 1, X, 11-13; Adams, *History of the United States*, VII, 128-30; Gilpin, *War of 1812*, pp. 217-19. For attack of Tecumseh on Procter see *Richardson's War of 1812*, ed. Casselman, pp. 204-07; cf. *Chronicles of Verchères de Boucherville*, ed. Quaife, pp. 141-43.

18. "Elliott to Claus, October 24, 1813," *Claus Papers*, MG 19, Series F 1, 111-13; *Richardson's War of 1812*, ed. Casselman, pp. 204-42; "Colonel Claus to Lieutenant Claus, May 11, 1814," *The Documentary History of the Campaigns upon the Niagara Frontier, 1812-1814*, ed. E. A. Cruikshank (Lundy's Lane Historical Society, *Publications*, III, parts I-IX, 1902-08), VIII, 168; C. O. Ermatinger, "The Retreat of Procter and Tecumseh," *Ontario Historical Society Papers and Records*, XVII (1919), 11-21.

19. Stanley, "Indians in the War of 1812," pp. 155-61; also Public Archives of Canada, Series C. Military, C 681, 4/1813 (letters of December 12, 17, 18, 20, 22), C 682, pp. 5-8; C 1219, pp. 160-61; *Documentary History of the Campaigns upon the Niagara Frontier*, ed. Cruikshank, IX, 32; Adams, *History of the United States*, VII, 202-03.

20. Public Archives of Canada, Series C. Military, C 682, pp. 100-03, 190, 192-95, 208-10; C 1222, pp. 48-50.

KENTUCKY IN THE NORTHWEST CAMPAIGN

Thomas D. Clark

ON JANUARY 3, 1809, Henry Clay, a member of the Kentucky House
of Representatives, introduced a resolution urging members of that
body to clothe themselves henceforth in fabrics of American manu-
facture.[1] The Fayette County farmer-lawyer had already prepared
for himself a suit out of his own Ashland Estate merino wool.[2] Two
years earlier, the House of Representatives, wrought up over the
Chesapeake-Leopard affair, had thrown reason to the wind and proposed to prohibit the citation of British statutes and judicial decisions. Lawyer Clay, who later became so vehement against British
textile manufacturers, called for moderation. He was willing to accept the compromise that no decisions rendered after July 4, 1776,
would be cited.[3]

Clay's homespun resolution came at a time when Kentuckians were
highly excited over Britain's imperious acts of impressment, the failures
of the various diplomatic missions, and the firing on the *Chesapeake.*
These emotional issues widened the political fissure between Kentucky's
Jeffersonian Republicans and the thinning ranks of Federalists. The most
outspoken of the latter was crotchety Humphrey Marshall of Frankfort.
Marshall regarded Clay's resolution and anti-British comments as bla-
tant demagoguery. In the arguments which ensued, Marshall called Clay
a liar and threatened physical violence in the assembly. A challenge to a
duel followed; the two antagonists met at Shippingport and crossed over
into the Indiana Territory to preserve their honor. Clay was wounded in
the thigh, but returned home a Republican hero—even though he and
Marshall were censured by the assembly for dueling.[4]

The Clay-Marshall duel may be considered the first shot in Kentucky's participation in the War of 1812. From the viewpoint of most
Kentuckians the war to come was in fact a Kentucky conflict. They
were aroused over the violations of neutrality on the seas, the Orders-
in-Council, the Napoleonic decrees, and subsequently the American

78

embargo and non-intercourse acts. Though Kentucky was far removed from the coast and the sea lanes, sea-going trade was vital to its economy. Since 1787, commerce down the Mississippi had been the lifeline of Kentucky farmers and merchants. Almost all Kentucky farm products that were sold outside the state went to market by way of the western rivers and the port of New Orleans. James Brown, Henry Clay's brother-in-law, wrote from Louisiana early in 1810, "Deeply interested as you must feel in the prosperity of Kentucky you cannot have overlooked the obvious fact that its safety; tranquility; wealth and even continuance of the form of government it enjoys depend on the destinies of the Mississippi. Should this key to your trade fall into the hands of either of the great nations who now figure on the European theatre, the effects would be serious if not ruinous to your prosperity."[5]

There was a lingering and deep fear in Kentucky of both the Indians and British in the Northwest. This grew out of the bitter revolutionary years when raiders of both groups crossed the Ohio to threaten every settlement from Logan's Fort to Boonesboro. When these halted there were still bitter attacks upon migrating settlers along the Ohio until Anthony Wayne's army pushed the Indian menace farther inland. This act, however, erased neither the sense of fear nor the deep hatreds which had developed over two decades.

A sense of expansion in every field of activity had characterized Kentucky at the turn of the nineteenth century. Her fields and pastures were reaching peaks of production. Still-houses, mills, smokehouses, and tiny factories loaded hundreds of flatboats each season with goods for the markets down stream. The trails and roads were crowded with hogs, cattle, and mules being driven to the eastern seaboard farms and markets.

Culturally, Kentucky was reaching a second stage of maturity. There had been a great religious revival, with its lingering results. As farm lands were brought into full cultivation, towns were expanding. Pioneers who had begun life west of the mountains in log houses were now building new brick houses. There was a phenomenal expansion of population, an increase of two hundred per cent from 73,000 in 1792 to 220,955 in 1800; and again to 406,511 in 1810.[6] Kentuckians were restless people. Though they had found land and some wealth in the frontier state, many looked farther west to make their fortunes. Lands in Indiana, along the Wabash, in Illinois, and even beyond the Mississippi in the Louisiana Purchase, beckoned. Even the Northwest along the Great Lakes was in range. When Kentucky militiamen went out with Anthony Wayne in 1793 and 1794, they spied out the land as carefully as they searched for Indian villages.[7]

A burgeoning nationalism had beset Kentucky—a nationalism that blended "spread-eagleism" with Jeffersonian Republicanism, and was further spiced by thorough dislike of foreign snubbing of the United States. As early as December, 1808, Henry Clay had given voice to this kind of nationalistic viewpoint. He stirred his fellow legislators with a fervent denunciation of Britain and France, and held Jeffersonian Republicanism up to them as a source of national salvation. The General Assembly fell under his spell and resolved that it "would view with the utmost horror, a proposition in any shape to submit to the tributary exactions of Great Britain, as attempted to be enforced by her orders in council, or to acquiesce in the violations of neutral rights, as menaced by the French decrees; in resisting with oppressions they pledge themselves to the general government for their most energetic support."[8]

Less than a month later the legislators agreed that a strong garrison should be stationed at Michilimackinac on Lake Huron, at St. Louis, and at the confluence of the Ohio and Mississippi for the protection of New Orleans and the river trade. Such a plan would "enfeeble" any attempt of foreigners to invade the western country either from the Gulf or the Great Lakes.[9]

As news of the failures of the various British diplomatic missions to the United States appeared in the Kentucky newspapers, the nationalistic mutterings grew more audible. In January, 1810, the General Assembly stated its maturing views in a resolution denouncing the Jackson mission. The legislators agreed almost unanimously on the demand for withdrawal of "the said [British minister] Jackson, and that whatever may be the consequences resulting therefrom, the State of Kentucky will be ready to meet them and to see them to a conclusion."[10] Again the hand of Henry Clay was apparent. It became clear that Americans were taking up where they had left off in 1781. The task of establishing independence from the British empire remained to be finished. Sentiments expressed in Lexington, Louisville, and Frankfort might have come from Samuel Adams, James Otis, Patrick Henry, and Tom Paine.

As the issues of impressment, Orders-in-Council, Napoleonic decrees, and the embargoes became more involved, Kentuckians became more aroused. Precisely a month after the adoption of the anti-Jackson resolution, Henry Clay arose in the United States Senate, the freshest of junior senators, to make his maiden speech. He opposed lifting all restrictions on Britain, and no doubt this speech was the opening of his famous "War Hawk" campaign of 1811.[11] He was direct in his discussion of the possibility of war with Britain or France, and he pleaded with the central government to appropriate funds to maintain an adequate military force to protect the republic. "It is said, however, that no object is attainable by war with Britain," he told his colleagues. "In its fortunes we are to estimate not only the benefit to be derived to ourselves, but the injury to be done the enemy. The conquest of Canada is in your power. I trust I shall not be deemed presumptuous when I state, what I verily believe, that the militia of Kentucky are alone competent to place Montreal and upper Canada at your feet. Is it nothing to the British nation—is it nothing to the pride of her monarch to have the last of the immense North American possessions held by him in the commencement of his reign, wrested from his dominion? Is it nothing to us to extinguish the torch that lights up savage warfare? Is it nothing to acquire the entire fur trade connected with that country, and to destroy the temptation and opportunity of violating your revenue and other laws?"[12]

Before the fiery Kentucky senator returned to Washington the next year as a member of the House of Representatives, he had further stirred his fellow Kentuckians in the congressional campaign of 1811. His remark about the ability of the Kentucky militia to carry out the conquest of Canada was often quoted. However, Clay was unwilling to stop with Canada—there was a score to be settled along the Gulf. The Floridas should also be annexed. The Kemper brothers, Reuben, Samuel, and Nathan, had already stirred revolt at Baton Rouge in 1804 and again in 1810, and as a result President James Madison proclaimed the authority of the United States over West Florida to the Perdido River.[13] Madison's actions provoked debate in the Senate, with some senators pleading the justness of Spanish claims to West Florida. Speaking for the western point of view, in a vigorous and lengthy discourse, Clay condemned his fellow senators for their lack of boldness. "I am not, Sir, in favor of cherishing the passion of conquest. But I must be permitted to conclude by declaring my hope to see ere long, the *new* United States (if you will allow me the expression) embracing not only the old thirteen states, but the entire country east of the Mississippi, including East Florida and some of the territories to the north of us also."[14]

This tone pervaded the argument used by Clay and Richard M. Johnson in the congressional campaign. Returning from Washington after the adjournment of the Eleventh Congress, young Senator Clay, fresh from challenging his colleagues with his expansionist oratory, was now ready to take to the stump in the Bluegrass. Kentuckians everywhere were ready to go to war with Britain, with the Indians of the Northwest, with Spain, and even with France if it interfered with their trade and aspirations in the West. The opportunity for Kentuckians to test their fighting mettle was at hand—even nearer than most of the militant editors and orators suspected.[15]

Along the Wabash there was friction between the Shawnee Indians and their allies, and the encroaching white land speculators and settlers. Governor William Henry Harrison had successfully negotiated a series of treaties with the Indians pertaining to lands on the Wabash, but he had failed to establish a basis for the successful and peaceful co-occupation of the country. Above all, the Indian treaty made in 1809 had failed to accomplish its objectives. Tecumseh and the Prophet, with their villages, prevented peaceful withdrawal of the tribes.

Although Kentucky had no direct interest in the Wabash Indian disputes, and the Indian unrest in this area failed to offer any direct threat to the commonwealth, its reaction was strong. Ancient and lingering fears were revived. The belief was widespread that the British were again supplying the Indians with arms and encouraging them to thwart the expanding frontier settlements.[16] At almost the same moment that Senator Clay was returning from Washington, a detachment of more than a hundred Kentuckians were on their way from Louisville to join William Henry Harrison on the Wabash. Among these volunteers were General Samuel Wells, Colonel Joseph Hamilton Daviess, Colonel Abraham Owens, and a Colonel Keiger. In the Battle of Tippecanoe, Colonel Daviess and Colonel Owens were killed, along with several private soldiers from the ranks of the Kentucky volunteers.[17]

This was Kentucky's first disturbing loss in the new conflict. At Frankfort members of the General Assembly agreed to wear crepe on their left arm for thirty days, "in testimony of their deep regrets for the loss of the brave and meritorious Colonels Daviess and Owens, and the other volunteers from Kentucky who fell in battle."[18] In January of that year legislators announced their disdain for Great Britain and proclaimed that Kentuckians were second to none in their patriotism. The state was declared ready to expend the last mite of its energy to resist the "unnatural" enemy, so long as Britain continued to disregard the rights of the United States. War at that point appeared inevitable, and the legislature accepted the challenge of blood.[19]

Kentuckians looked forward to a declaration of war by the fall of 1811. From almost every political stump orators pleaded for a reckoning through war. "Savage Britain" had already offended in the *Chesapeake-Leopard* debacle and through the arrogance of its diplomats in Washington; at Tippecanoe ancient Indian enemies had used British guns, tomahawks, and knives. Editors filled their columns with news from Washington and the Northwest frontier.[20] Much of this oratory was strongly tinctured with Kentucky politics. Occasionally Republicans whipped the dry hides of the Federalist guard, but new antagonists had appeared. A cry went up to bring Isaac Shelby, the old Revolutionary hero, out of retirement and to again make him governor.[21] Robert Wickliffe wrote to Henry Clay on May 31, 1812: "Shelby is a candidate & will beat Slaughter but cant you help him by making some statement in the *Intelligencer* which will be copied here. In which you may state the military ardour of the state & something handsome of Shelby as a military man & the hopes that America will indulge from Kentucky such a commander-in-chief of her militia."[22]

The war fever during the gubernatorial campaign of 1812 could not disguise the partisan nature of the campaign. Another Kentuckian, of much narrower Republican stripe than Robert Wickliffe, attacked Shelby under the pseudonym of "Abinidah Hardwood." He opposed the old warhorse's taking the field, writing: "A set of men, who, after having damned our Jefferson, Madison, and the whole people, with every proceeding of our government, into the deep abyss, now grasp for the loaves and fishes of that very administration, which, with the proceeding breath they execrated!! To be sure, Old Daddy Shelby must once more, in his dotage, be trickled forth into the governorship to help his tory lineage to some handsome appointment or other."[23]

In the opening session of the Twelfth Congress Henry Clay was elected Speaker of the House of Representatives. He and his War Hawk colleagues helped push the nation rapidly toward a declaration of war. Back in Kentucky the press carried every shred of news available about the crisis. Harrison's campaign along the Wabash was reviewed and memorialized. The debates in Congress were reported in full. The preparation and march of General William Hull's army was news of the most exciting nature. From May to August, 1812, every courier returning from the Northwest brought news of what was happening along that frontier. Whether editors interpreted the news or not, their stories were highly optimistic. Both editors and orators strove mightily to develop a heroic image of the Kentuckian. They wrote and spoke of bravery in battle as a natural attribute of their people.[24]

The editors wrote in almost precisely the same vein as their forbears who denounced Britain in the 1770's, emphasizing patriotism, personal bravery, the necessity of combating the tyrant's yoke, and referring to the manifest destiny of American civilization. Characteristic of this sentiment were the words of the aging Judge Samuel McDowell of Mercer County. In 1814 he wrote to his son-in-law, Andrew Reid of Rockbridge County, Virginia: "I declare I would never Buy a Peace at the Expense of one foot of territory nor have the Indians Even Named in a treaty of Peice with England. I did not think that it was Proper to have declared the War at the time it was done when I considered that we were unprepared for it, having been in no way Prepared to have Immediately Carried into Effect. But I would if possable have such an Army now as would by the Blessing of God take the Canadys in three months next campaign. I'd have at least One hundred and fifty thousand men in the field and at least 100,000 of them for Canady. And never stop till Both the Canadys were taken and exclude the British from North America altogether. . . ."[25]

On May 12, Governor Charles Scott called for volunteers to fill Kentucky's quota of fifty-five hundred men out of the one hundred thousand to be recruited in the nation. The causes of the coming war, Governor Scott told prospective volunteers, "are to be found in the blood of our unoffending brethren—in the groans and stripes of thousands of our countrymen, impressed and confined at this moment in the floating dungeons, forced to turn their arms against the country which gave them birth, and friends and relatives dear to their hearts. Rise in the majesty of freemen—regard as enemies the enemies of your country. Remember the Spirit of '76." Then he appealed forcefully to their state pride: "Let not Kentucky at least, amongst the foremost in patriotism and Republican pride, need a draft to fill her quota. Let us teach the world there is a difference between freemen fighting for their rights, and subjects fighting to gratify the lust or ambition of masters."[26]

On June 30, 1812, news of the declaration of war reached Lexington and central Kentucky. Cannon were fired to celebrate the long-anticipated news. In Nicholasville, Winchester, and Richmond, Senator John Pope was hanged in effigy because he had voted against war.[27] In the noise and excitement of the patriotic furor it seems that no one took seriously the War Department's listing of goods needed by Kentucky's fifty-five hundred volunteers.[28] Perhaps it was unfortunate that the first call for troops came during the warmth of summer; too little attention was given the realities of a lake-shore winter in Michigan. In fact, the foolish optimism which prevailed convinced everybody that the Kentuckians would be home by the first frost. Before the end of November the volunteers were suffering desperately from lack of adequate clothing and shoes.[29]

Never before in the history of the state had Kentuckians been subjected to so much fervent patriotic oratory as from May, 1812, to February, 1813. In late May the Forty-second Regular militia paraded through the streets of Lexington. The youthful lawyer John Jordan Crittenden addressed the troops in front of the courthouse. He reviewed the state's militant heritage, made the anvil ring for Jeffersonian Republicanism, damned the grasping and doddering British monarchy, and described the barbarities of unrestrained Indian warfare. When he had finished, the drums rolled and volunteers stepped forward. Enough men volunteered to exceed the local quota for defense of the republic and Republicanism.[30]

No public occasion aroused more enthusiasm than did the celebration at Maxwell Springs in Lexington on the Fourth of July. A throng followed a patriotic parade from Main Street to the famous political hustings ground, where orators raised the war whoop and made the eagle scream. To conclude this occasion, eighteen fervent toasts were drunk. The celebrants figuratively bared their teeth at Indians and British with such sentiments as "Our volunteers—Ready to avenge the wrongs and vindicate the right of their country—the spirit of Montgomery will lead them to victory on the Plains of Abraham."[31] They had praise for that master jingoist, Congressman Clay, and another slight for John Pope. They drank to "Our immediate Representative in Congress—Henry Clay—in supporting the declaration of war—he was indeed our representative."[32]

Henry Clay's Kentucky colleagues in the Twelfth Congress, Samuel Hopkins, Richard M. Johnson, William P. Duvall, Samuel McKee, and Thomas Montgomery, volunteered for service in the Northwest. It was said that they were ready for action all the way from Lexington to the Plains of Abraham. Even Thomas Smith, editor of the *Kentucky Gazette,* became so aroused over the news which appeared in the columns of his paper that he left the cares of the editorial desk and type stick to others and rode off to fight for American liberty in the second great war for independence.[33]

While war fever was high, and more volunteers came forward than could be accepted, the news from the Northwestern front turned sour. Reports from General William Hull's army as it made its laborious way across Ohio and Michigan had been cheerful. Weekly courier reports of the General's activities had built up optimistic expectations. Indeed, it seemed from these early reports that the Americans were well on their way across Canada. Then in August came the jarring rumor that all was not well.[34] On August 16 the army was surrendered.[35] Now the war promised to be more than an oratorical orgy in which a new generation of Kentuckians would have to prove the truth of the toast: "The American Flag—it has fifteen stripes for its enemies; fifteen stars of glory for its brave defenders."[36]

Before news of General Hull's surrender reached Kentucky the first contingent of two thousand men had left Georgetown for Newport. Here they assembled before crossing the Ohio River to join other American militiamen at Fort Wayne. On hand at Georgetown to address the volunteers as they prepared for their long march were the Reverend James Blythe, President of Transylvania University, and Henry Clay. Reverend Blythe prayed earnestly for their success, while Henry Clay explained the reasons for war. In one of his famous flourishes, Clay said that the volunteers were to remember that "Kentucky was famed for her bravery!—they had the double character of Americans and Kentuckians to support." This challenging note was to serve as the order-of-the-day issued by General William Lewis just before the Battle of the Raisin.[37] At the moment Blythe and Clay spoke, General Hull was surrendering his army at Detroit.[38]

Early preparations for war were not without political implications. William Henry Harrison went to Kentucky in August, 1812, to confer with Henry Clay and Isaac Shelby. He quickly won the confidence of these men, and that of the Kentucky public. His leadership at Tippecanoe had stamped him as an old-line frontier Indian fighter. In commenting on the flood of public resolutions which resulted from every public assembly, Henry Clay observed that one such resolution "affirmed our ability to bring the Indian war to a speedy conclusion under the guidance of William Henry Harrison."[39]

Before the Kentucky volunteers left the Georgetown assembly ground, Governor Isaac Shelby began to wonder whether the War Department would keep its promise to have supplies on hand at Newport. Communications between Kentucky and Washington were slow, and Shelby had no assurance that Dr. William Eustis understood that the Americans were fighting a subtle and wary enemy. Everything necessary to equip Hull's army was purchased after marching orders had been issued. Only with the aid of individuals equipping themselves and of ladies making tents and other supplies were the Kentuckians able to march in August.

There was also confusion at the Newport rendezvous over the promise to pay the troops two months' pay and an additional sum of $16.00 in lieu of clothing. In order to facilitate matters, Governor Shelby proposed the appointment of a western military board with powers of decision over such vital matters.[40]

In time Shelby's anxiety increased, as the central government failed to produce the necessary supplies. He delayed further movement of Kentucky troops, and turned away eager volunteers who were unable to feed and equip themselves.[41] He did this despite the fact that there was bustling activity in the state's homes, farms, and small factories to supply the necessary clothing and equipment.

Kentucky lay in the middle of a sprawling arc of Indian frontier which reached from the Great Lakes to the Alabama and Mississippi Territories. The frontier along the lower Wabash and on into Illinois promised serious troubles. The state was called upon to assemble two thousand men about Vincennes.[42] To command this sector, Governor Shelby turned to Congressman Samuel Hopkins, who had come home from Washington to resume his rank as general of the militia. Shelby informed Hopkins that this crisis called for the services of Kentucky's most experienced military leaders.[43] Hopkins was instructed to assemble his army at Louisville and to march it westward to the Wabash. The general was then to push on to Vincennes and Kaskaskia while Harrison hurried off to Detroit. General William Russell, with another command of Kentuckians, would move into the Illinois country toward the Illinois River.[44]

General Hopkins acted with dispatch; by September 26, he had assembled an army of thirty-day volunteers in Louisville. Governor Shelby wrote General Harrison: "I have never seen such a body of men in the western country or anywhere else."[45] Hopkins and his men followed George Rogers Clark's old route, but hardly his path to glory. By the first of November the expedition was known to be a failure. It exhausted its supplies and time, failed to find the Kickapoo and Peoria Indians, and above all, lost its courage. The Indians set the prairie on fire and drove the Kentuckians back. Again Shelby wrote Harrison, but this time he said: "This [failure of the Hopkins expedition] has ended an enterprise on which the flower of Kentucky had enlisted themselves and are now returning home deeply mortified by disappointment." A week later the Governor's disappointment had turned to burning anger. "This event," he wrote Harrison, "has terminated most dishonorably to the volunteers. I have no doubt but this refractory conduct in turning back contrary to the General's consent will be found to be owing to the secret plotting of some, who may yet be little suspected, but who I hope will be discovered and placed in their true colors. . . . I am surprised that among the great number of influential and eloquent & respectable characters who composed the army, that scores of them did not turn out of the ranks and exert every power to prevent the disgraceful retreat they were about to make."[46]

War came not only to the male population; Kentucky women attempted to serve the needs of the army from the Kentucky fireside. Spinning wheels and looms were busy preparing cloth, socks, coats, blankets, and shirts. Everywhere the whir of the wheel or the clatter of the loom vied with the orators to prove that mothers and daughters were again ready to support their men in war. Letters which came back from the Michigan front described the needs for warm clothing. Bitter cold chilled the volunteers who had rushed away from home in July and August little anticipating the ordeal of a northern winter. The toll of sickness and exposure was almost as heavy as loss from actual combat. Volunteers sent back graphic accounts of the suffering of their comrades from illness and cold. They ate poor food and drank water from stagnant puddles, including wagon ruts; their feet were frostbitten as they walked and rode from one station to another; they gorged themselves on too much green corn from Indian fields in the summer and ate too much fresh meat in the winter.[47] Medical care was almost nonexistent and, more often than not, of the folk-Indian variety.

The troops who marched away from Georgetown in August, 1812, were commanded by Brigadier General John Payne; the regiments were commanded by Colonel John Allen, Colonel M. Scott, and Colonel William Lewis.[48] There were more than two thousand men in this contingent destined to join the commands of General James Winchester and General William Henry Harrison in Michigan. For reasons which may reflect as much the willfulness and lack of discipline of the troops as the personal and military deficiencies of General Winchester, the Kentuckians looked upon service in his command as distasteful. Before most of the troops volunteered for service they had heard much of the bravery and gallantry of William Henry Harrison. Editor, politician, and orator all proclaimed him as a man of the frontier whose character embodied all the virtues of the West. To serve under him was one of the glories of the war. The Kentucky General Assembly believed "That in the late campaign against the Indians upon the Wabash, Governor William H. Harrison has, in the opinion of the Legislature, behaved like a hero, a patriot and a general:—and that for his cool, deliberate, skilful and gallant conduct in the late battle of Tippecanoe, he well deserves the warmest thanks of the nation."[49]

General Winchester may have incurred the enmity of the Kentuckians in another way. He was not in favor with the predominant Kentucky political forces. In the field, troops played pranks on him, violated his orders, and were otherwise obstreperous. A private soldier wrote that "I always had some misgivings about Winchester's Success with his Army Knowing that he was not loved by his men, for they all despised him, and were continually playing some tricks of[f] on him. At one encampment, they killed a porcupine and skined it and stretched the Skin over a pole that he used for a particular purpose in the night, and he went and sat down on it, and it like to have ruined him. At another Encampment they sawed his pole that he had for the same purpose nearly in two, so that when he went to use it in the night it broke intoo and let his generalship, Uniform and all fall Backwards in no very decent place, for I seen his Regimentals hanging high upon a place the next day taking the fresh air."[50] When the Kentuckians arrived at Fort Wayne they discovered that Harrison had given up command of the troops to Winchester. Benjamin Logan, a private soldier, wrote Miss Jane Allen of Shelbyville that this was much against the wishes of the whole army.[51]

In the fall of 1812 the Kentuckians were widely dispersed. Some were at Fort Wayne, some at Fort Defiance, and others were assaulting scattered Indian villages, destroying crops and supplies.[52] As early as October, most of them began to face the realities of the war. Colonel John Allen wrote his family that they had beef without bread, and poor, unsalted beef at that. There were rumors that the troops might be left to starve. The weather was cool, and many soldiers were barefoot and without blankets. "Think of those men doing duty on guard at night in this northern climate where the frosts have already nearly stripped the trees of their leaves—Yet they say that they are willing and anxious to proceed."[53] A month later the Colonel wrote his wife that he wanted her to have a local cobbler make a pair of boots for him. "I want them large," he told her, "so as to take in a coarse stocking. . . . The boots are the most important, for this country is so flat that the water is frequently over shoes and my present boots will not last much longer & indeed are unfit for the service."[54]

This was the story of life in the Michigan country for the Kentuckians. They lacked food, clothing, and proper shelter, and they were bored with the indecision which had bogged the army down. Elias Darnell, a private soldier, reported there was even a threat of mutiny and that John Haggard was drummed out of camp for his demoralizing activities. General Winchester had difficulty enforcing his orders against random firing of guns. At Christmas time troops were twice called out and marched because of irresponsible firing in celebration of the holidays.[55]

The bitterly cold winter set in in November, 1812, and by December the movement of boats on the rivers became impossible. On December 21, Winchester ordered his short-term troops to ready themselves for movement to the Maumee Rapids. Sleds were prepared, to be pulled by packhorses and even by soldiers.[56] By December 30 the troops were ready to advance. Snow fell to a depth of two feet, temporarily halting the march. Thus, in a series of starts and stops, the Kentuckians pressed on to the River Raisin, Frenchtown, and disaster.

By January 11 the British and Indians knew of the presence of Winchester's forces. Colonel John Allen wrote his wife on January 13 that the troops had reached the foot of the Maumee Rapids and had gone into camp. He was weary of slow movements which got nowhere, but he expected action soon.[57] Four days later Robert Logan wrote: "The British and Indians are apprised of our arrival at this place and have commenced destroying and carrying off the property of the inhabitants on the River Raison about 7 o'clock last night it is about 35 miles from this place at sunrise this morning a detachment under Colonel Lewis started and I am in hopes will at least be able to protect the poor defenseless inhabitants from entire destruction. I think you may expect to hear of bloody work shortly."[58]

Logan's words were indeed prophetic. The story of the attack at Frenchtown and the succeeding massacre along the Raisin is well known. When news of the Frenchtown-Raisin disaster reached Kentucky, Governor Isaac Shelby was attending a theatrical performance. "He was called out," said a news story, "and of course, the news soon spread through the house; at the conclusion of the third act, the whole audience had retired. Here you see fathers going about half distracted, while mothers, wives and sisters are weeping at home. The voice of lamentation is loud! Distress is deep: yet neither public nor private distress can damp the ardor of the people. Already they propose to raise a new army to revenge the loss of their brave countrymen."[59]

Kentucky's first answer to the disaster at the Raisin was the mustering of four regiments, a total of three thousand men. These were dispatched for the Northwest under the command of General Green Clay on April 12,[60] and reached Fort Defiance on May 4—a much faster march than had heretofore been made by Kentuckians. Late in February Richard M. Johnson was given permission to raise a regiment of mounted Kentucky volunteers to go to the rescue of the Northwest.[61] Johnson's regiment was at the place of rendezvous in Newport on May 22, and on June 7 had arrived at Fort Wayne.[62]

More dramatic was the decision of Isaac Shelby to personally lead a command of Kentucky volunteers to the Northwest. William Henry Harrison sent his aide de camp, David Trimble, to Kentucky in July, 1813, to confer with the Governor. In the desperate situation in Michigan, Shelby must have sensed once again the challenge which three decades before had sent a rowdy band of frontiersmen rushing into battle against the British Ferguson at King's Mountain. Shelby was a Lincoln County farmer who, like Cincinnatus, had been called from the furrow in time of great need. Upon his return to office, he wrote Governor William Blount of Tennessee that he felt he had been on the farm too long to again assume responsibility for the complex duties of a chief magistrate.[63]

Governor Harrison's letter contained both a note of pessimism and a challenge. It was mid-summer, late indeed to call up militia, but there was immediate need for troops. He suggested that Shelby call for from four hundred to two thousand volunteers. The Governor felt he saw victory in the near future if he could secure men and arms. Then he appealed to Shelby's vanity: "To make this last effort, why not, dear sir, come in person—you would not object to a command that would be nominal only; I have such confidence in your wisdom, that you in fact should be the guiding head, and I the hand. The situation you would be placed in is not without parallel: Scipio, the conqueror of Carthage, did not disdain to act as the lieutenant of his younger and less experienced brother Lucius."[64]

Harrison's note struck fire. On August 1 Governor Shelby appealed to his fellow Kentuckians to meet him at Newport on the last day of that month.[65] He wrote Harrison that he proposed to lead the troops himself.[66] To his fellow Kentuckians he said: "I have appointed the 31st day of August next, at New Port, for a general rendezvous of Kentucky volunteers. I will meet you there in person. I will lead you to the field of battle, and share with you the dangers and honors of the campaign." In an optimistic vein he predicted that they would not be gone more than sixty days. Indeed, Scipio was off to serve Lucius.[67] Shelby and his volunteers were in camp at Upper Sandusky on September 12, 1813; early in November he was back in the governor's office in Frankfort immediately following the battle of the Thames.

Johnson's gallant "forlorn hope" brought glory to the Kentuckians. William Whitley, a famous old pioneer, fell in the famous sortie, and Richard M. Johnson was wounded. An argument was begun which can never be settled. There were those who swore that Whitley killed Tecumseh; others contended with equal vigor that Richard M. Johnson killed him. In reporting the victory on the Thames to Congress, President James Madison, after praising William Henry Harrison, said: "To Colonel Johnson and his mounted volunteers, whose impetuous onset gave a decisive blow to the ranks of the enemy, and to the spirit of the volunteer militia . . . who bore an interesting part in the scene; more especially to the chief magistrate of Kentucky, at the head of them, whose heroism signalized in the war which established the independence of his country, sought at an advanced age a share in hardships and battles for maintaining its rights and safety."[68]

More important than either the causes or the actual fighting were the results of the War of 1812. There is no doubt that local factional and national partisan politics played a large part in persuading the people to march off to war with such enthusiasm in 1812. The state's pride was injured by the failure of General Hull's mission, and the disaster at the Raisin was more than an injury to pride—it brought grief to many Kentucky homes. Never before had there been so fine an opportunity for a rising generation of ambitious young politicians to establish themselves in the public minds as hero figures. From

Henry Clay to the lowest local magistrate, they made a rich political asset of the war. Congressmen who rushed home from Washington to join the volunteers were among the first to establish their names as heroes.

The first generation of Kentuckians after the pioneers felt a need to prove itself worthy of its descent; it would open the way into a new western frontier. Where their fathers had opened the Kentucky country at high costs of hardship and sacrifice, the younger men would push the rim of Indian and British occupation farther and farther back. They even thought of pushing the British and the Spanish off the North American continent altogether. Despite the fact that volunteers went into military service for thirty-, sixty-, and ninety-day periods, the individual volunteer thought of himself as a full-blown hero at the moment of his enlistment. In many respects the war was for the Kentuckian a rejuvenation of spirit. Just as there had been a great revival of evangelical religion in Cane Ridge at the turn of the century, there was a rebirth of patriotism in 1812. More important, the economy of Kentucky had so developed that everybody thought in terms of a widening market facility. In few places in the country had farmers received a richer return from their lands.

There was every reason to believe that the West was rapidly becoming the center of national expansion. Land-hungry people as well as speculators looked to the widening rim of the frontier for new lands which could be opened to exploitation. Kentucky rode a wave of prosperity from 1800 to 1812. Fear that British maritime impressment and interference with American trade would depress the prices of western farm products caused many Kentuckians to favor war. Mills were built on almost every creek where there was current enough to turn millstones. Ever-increasing crops of grain were being turned into meal, flour, and distilled spirits for the downriver trade. Merchants flocked to Lexington, Louisville, and the smaller county-seat towns. At the very moment that Joseph H. Daviess and his Kentucky companions were fighting Indians on Tippecanoe Creek, the *New Orleans* was in Louisville awaiting water conditions favorable to crossing the Falls of the Ohio.[69] Even the most skeptical soon saw in the success of the steamboat a new era in the navigation of the western waters. It would be hard to separate a note of economic and social optimism from the enormous outburst of militant and patriotic enthusiasm. Politically, Kentuckians felt that success of the Jeffersonian Republican Party also reflected their own rising influence in the expanding nation.

From the ranks of the volunteers who marched off to the Wabash, to Michigan, and to New Orleans, came the largest output of heroes that ever returned to Kentucky after a war. Henry Clay, as a provocator of war and then as a peacemaker, remained a leading figure in Kentucky politics without benefit of uniform or battle experience. Richard M. Johnson, whether he killed Tecumseh or not, rode home from the Thames a major political figure who ultimately became Vice-President of the United States. John Adair came home from New Orleans to be elected governor. Out of the ranks came state legislators, judges, diplomatic officials, congressmen, United States senators, territorial governors, and secretaries. None won more enthusiastic acclaim than Isaac Shelby. The sixty-three-year-old governor returned to Frankfort in November to resume the duties of governor which he had left in July. The General Assembly was unreserved in expressing "the high estimation in which they hold the late conduct of the chief magistrate ISAAC SHELBY, in leading the Kentucky militia into upper Canada, to victory and glory."[70]

Along with the political hopefuls, who hardly got home before entering political races, there came the self-anointed heroes who never forgot their glorious feats along the Raisin, at Fort Meigs, at Fort Stephenson, at Put-in-Bay, at the Thames, and at New Orleans. Four or five of these thought well enough of their exploits to write their memoirs after the war.[71] One spokesman will suffice here for all the veterans. In 1862 Tarrance Kirby, a time-worn but mellow veteran of the Thames and New Orleans, made a request of his country. He asked President Abraham Lincoln to take his heroism into account and release his Confederate grandsons from federal prisoner-of-war camps.

"We the undersigned," he wrote, "respectfully petition your honor that some twelve months ago my grandsons William Bradley & Van Fulgium was captured by the Federal Soldiers—and are at this time in prison at Camp Morton Ind. at the time they were captured they wer on there way home having served out there time in the Rebble army—and was likely to be conscripted whech they wer vary much opposed to. He is vary desieras to take the Amnester Oath give bond and return home and live a quiet sitizen. They are the Grand children of the Old Hero that served his country in the War of 1812. Four companies to rescue the Bleeding Fruntiers of Michigan and Ohio—while Indians was yelling around my Ears like Ten Thousand Wild Panthers in the woods swearing in Indian Language that they would have my scelp or hear before day—or make ther Hatchets drunk in my Blood—but bore it with corage and fortitude I foute the First Battle at Tippecanoe and the Second Battle at the River Reasen then drove the Indians frum ther to detroit—then across the river to Canida, then drove Proctor & Elliott from Mauldin to Moravian-town—then I shouted Triumph Victory over Proctor & Elliott and Tecumseh whole torso. I hope kill Tecumseh and *hope Skin him* and brot Two pieces of his yellow hide home with me to my Mother & Sweet Harts after a few days rest—ther was a call for volunteers to defend N Orleans I volunteered at the first tap of the drum under the immortal Andrew Jackson—I fought the Battle of 8th January & was wounded—throwed them Head and Heels cross file, they covered 10 Acres with death Blood and Wounds, and sent them Home with a dabsend to Old England which made a Mash of Lord Wellington's Army and when they got there they could not tell the news."[72]

Approximately sixty-five Kentuckians were slaughtered in the River Raisin massacre on the morning of January 22.[73] There can be no dependable estimate of the total number of men who lost their lives in battle or due to illness, exposure and accidents. Between 1811 and 1815, 25,695 men saw service in the armed forces. Long before the war was over, responsible Kentuckians learned that short-term militia service was a liability. They had made sadly erroneous guesses as to the effectiveness of militiamen against Indian and British forces. This faulty speculation had caused ninety per cent of the human suffering experienced in the war.[74] It may well have been one of the reasons for Winchester's haste before Frenchtown: the period of enlistment of his men was rapidly coming to an end.[75]

The Kentucky militia system was fundamentally weak. First, it was not selective of the men who went directly into a campaign where at any moment a battle situation might develop. General Samuel Hopkin's command of two thousand troops contained many men who no doubt were physically and emotionally unfitted for such an under-taking. Discipline was difficult, if not impossible to maintain. Even if a majority of the volunteers could be disciplined, the short terms of enlistment did not permit proper training by which raw recruits could be co-ordinated into efficient fighting units. Officers were as green and inexperienced as the recruits. Most of them attained their positions either by having organized companies and regiments, or by popular election.[76] In some cases men served alternately as officers and private soldiers.[77]

Equally as important were difficulties of supply. There were no means by which Kentucky could finance an expensive military ex-pedition out of its severely limited state budget, or by which it could raise funds by borrowing on such short notice. Even had there been money available, there were no organized facilities for creating and transporting arms and ammunition to the field. Clothing, foodstuffs, and hospital supplies were insufficient. No matter how willing quartermasters were, they too were inexperienced. Time was too short for them to organize their service, make contracts with local suppliers, and deliver goods five hundred miles over impossible roads.[78]

Legislators in Frankfort, and orating citizens elsewhere in Kentucky, when they thought of fighting the war, thought of the paunchy militiamen who paraded periodically on local muster grounds. Militiamen in turn believed the orators without stopping to consider what war really is. No public official in Kentucky in 1812 had dealt with a public emergency which required the appropriation of so large a sum of money, or the levying of enough taxes to finance such an emergency. The legislature was in the control of landholders who kept taxes low. In all the war talk between 1809 and 1814, there was remarkably little sense of what it would cost to finance Kentucky's activities in the Northwest.[79]

There is no doubt of the personal bravery of most of the Kentucky officers and troops who went off to fight in Michigan. They believed they could win the war, and were highly chagrined at the two setbacks before the Battle of the Thames. The Battle of the Thames itself proved their determination and personal bravery. Kentucky's military activities, however, could hardly be classed as of major strategic importance. Men who came home as recognized heroes earned their laurels as individuals who performed daring acts, rather than as members of units which made hard drives against an established line. Militarily, the Raisin and the Thames were repetitions of skirmishes against Indians and British which had first occurred when Daniel Boone's scouting party was attacked in the spring of 1775—the so-called Twetty's defeat.

In a broader sense, the War of 1812 led Kentucky into a ruinous course of economic inflation. Productive facilities were hardly organized and brought into the initial phases of efficient operation before the war was ended. When peace was restored there was lack of demand to consume the output of goods. Speculators, a term which described thousands of Kentuckians, threw caution aside and incurred debts in the purchase of lands, goods, and machines. They rode the wave of inflation with a sense that it was a promise of the future. Within five years after the end of the war the biting panic of 1819 not only wiped away economic gains made during the war, but almost paralyzed the state itself.

NOTES

In documenting a paper of this kind it is difficult to refer specifically to all of the secondary sources which were read. Here are listed a few major sources which should be noticed: Robert M. McElroy, *Kentucky in the Nation's History* (New York, 1909); Lewis and Richard H. Collins, *History of Kentucky*, 2 vols. (Covington, Ky., 1874); Leland Winfield Meyer, *The Life and Times of Colonel Richard M. Johnson* (New York, 1932); Francis F. Beirne, *The War of 1812* (New York, 1949); Bennett H. Young, *The Battle of the Thames* (Louisville, 1903).

1. *House Journal*, Kentucky General Assembly, 1808-09 (Frankfort), p. 93.

2. Bernard Mayo, *Henry Clay Spokesman of the New West* (Boston, 1937), p. 334; *Acts*, Kentucky General Assembly, 1808-09 (Frankfort), pp. 133-34.

3. Mayo, *op. cit.*, p. 335; George D. Prentice, *Biography of Henry Clay* (New York, 1831), pp. 39-41.

4. "Henry Clay to Humphrey Marshall, January 4, 1809," "Henry Clay to Thomas Hart, Junior, January 4, 1809," "Humphrey Marshall to Henry Clay, January 4, 1809," "Henry Clay to James Clark, January 19, 1809," "James Johnson to Henry Clay, January 28, 1809," "William Taylor Barry to Henry Clay, January 29, 1809," *The Papers of Henry Clay*, ed. James F. Hopkins (Lexington, Ky., 1959), I, 387-402; *Journal*, Kentucky House of Representatives, 1808-09 (Frankfort), p. 103.

5. "James Brown to Henry Clay, February 26, 1810," *Papers*, ed. Hopkins, I, 452-55.

6. Richard H. Collins, *History of Kentucky*, 2 vols. (Covington, Ky., 1874), I, 22, 25, 26.

7. William E. Connelley and E. M. Coulter, *History of Kentucky*, 5 vols. (Chicago, 1922), I, 376-89; Mann Butler, *History of the Commonwealth of Kentucky* (Louisville, 1834), pp. 235-57.

8. *Acts*, Kentucky General Assembly, 1808-09 (Frankfort, December 16, 1808), p. 129.

9. *Ibid.* (January 18, 1809), pp. 131-32.

10. *Ibid.* (January 22, 1810), p. 167.

11. Henry Clay was actually serving his second term in the Senate. He was first appointed to that body to serve out the unexpired term of John Adair, 1806-07. Mayo, *op. cit.*, pp. 244-302.

12. "Speech on the Proposed Repeal of the Non-Intercourse Act, February 22, 1810," *Papers*, ed. Hopkins, I, 448-52.

13. J. D. Richardson, *Papers and Messages of the Presidents of the United States*, 10 vols. (Washington, 1896-99), I, 480-81.

14. "Speech on the Occupation of West Florida, December 28, 1810," *Papers*, ed. Hopkins, I, 507-16; *Annals of Congress*, 12th Congress, 3rd Series, XXII, 55-64.

15. *Annals of Congress*, 11th Congress (February 22, 1810), 2nd Series, XXII, 579-82.

16. Connelley and Coulter, *op. cit.*, I, 547-48.

17. Robert B. McAfee, *History of the War in the Western Country* (Lexington, 1816), pp. 18-40.

18. *Acts*, Kentucky General Assembly (December 11, 1811), p. 252.

19. *Ibid.* (January 13, 1811), pp. 252-54.

20. *Kentucky Gazette* (November, 1811-October, 1813); *Lexington Observer* (November, 1811-October, 1813).

21. *Kentucky Gazette* (May 19, 1812).

22. "Robert Wickliffe to Henry Clay, May 31, 1812," *Papers,* ed. Hopkins, I, 664.

23. *Kentucky Gazette* (July 21, 1812).

24. *Ibid.* (May 12, 1812).

25. Samuel McDowell Collection, Filson Club, Louisville, Ky., September 25, 1783 to November 25, 1814. The specific letter cited above is "Samuel McDowell to Andrew Reid, November 25, 1814."

26. *Kentucky Gazette* (May 12, 1812).

27. *Ibid.* (June 20, 1812).

28. *Ibid.* (May 12, 1812).

29. McAfee, *op. cit.,* pp. 104-43; William B. Northcutt, *Diary* (original in Kentucky Historical Society), pp. 21-38; William Atherton, *Narrative and Suffering of the North-Western Army, Under General Winchester* (Frankfort, Ky., 1842), pp. 13-19, 24-32; Elias Darnell, *A Journal Containing an Accurate and Interesting Account of the Hardships, Sufferings, Battles, Defeat, and Captivity of those Heroic Kentucky Volunteers and Regulars Commanded by General Winchester in the Years, 1812 1813* (Philadelphia, 1854), pp. 37-41.

30. *Kentucky Gazette* (May 26, 1812).

31. *Ibid.* (July 7, 1812).

32. *Ibid.*

33. *Ibid.* (August 18, 1812).

34. *Ibid.* (August 25, September 1, and September 8, 1812).

35. *Ibid.* (September 8, 1812).

36. *Ibid.* (August 4, 1812).

37. "Speech to Troops at Georgetown, Kentucky, August 16, 1812," *Papers,* ed. Hopkins, I, 715.

38. Connelley and Coulter, *op. cit.,* I, 553; "Speech to Troops at Georgetown, Kentucky, August 16, 1812," *Papers,* ed. Hopkins, I, 715.

39. "Henry Clay to James Monroe, August 12, 1812," *Papers,* ed. Hopkins, I, 713.

40. Isaac Shelby, "Isaac Shelby to Secretary of War William Eustis, August 12, 1812," *Letter Book A,* Kentucky Historical Society (Frankfort).

41. *Ibid.,* "Isaac Shelby to General Green Clay, September 16, 1812."

42. *Ibid.,* "Isaac Shelby to General Winlock, August 30, 1812."

43. *Ibid.,* "Isaac Shelby to General Samuel Hopkins, September 8, 1812."

44. Collins, *op. cit.,* I, 696.

45. Shelby, "Isaac Shelby to William Henry Harrison, September 26, 1812," *Letter Book A.*

46. *Ibid.,* "Isaac Shelby to William Henry Harrison, November 7, 1812."

47. Northcutt, *Diary,* pp. 17-18; "Robert Logan to Mrs. James Allen, September 19, 1812," *Allen Papers,* University of Kentucky Archives (Lexington).

48. Robert Peter, *History of Fayette County, Kentucky* (Chicago, 1882), pp. 420-25; *Military History of Kentucky* (Frankfort, 1939), p. 80.

49. *Acts,* Kentucky General Assembly (January 13, 1812), p. 255.

50. Northcutt, *Diary,* p. 35.

51. "Robert Logan to Miss Jane Allen, September 19, 1812," *Allen Papers,* University of Kentucky Archives.

52. Anderson Chenault Quisenberry, *Kentucky in the War of 1812* (Frankfort, 1915), pp. 16-26; *Military History of Kentucky,* pp. 80-85.

53. "John Allen to Jane Allen, October 15, 1812," *Allen Papers.*

54. "John Allen to Jane Allen, November 19, 1812," *Allen Papers.*

55. Darnell, *op. cit.,* p. 40.

56. Atherton, *op. cit.,* pp. 26-27.

57. "John Allen to Jane Allen, January 13, 1813," *Allen Papers.*

58. "Robert Logan to Jane Allen, January 17, 1813," *Allen Papers.*

59. *Niles' Weekly Register,* III (February 13, 1813), 397.

60. *Military History of Kentucky,* pp. 84-85.

61. Meyer, *op. cit.,* p. 101.

62. *Ibid.,* pp. 110, 114.

63. Shelby, "Isaac Shelby to William Blount, October 31, 1812," *Letter Book A.*

64. *Journal,* Kentucky House of Representatives (Frankfort, 1813), p. 16.

65. Shelby, "Isaac Shelby to Militiamen of Kentucky, July 31, 1813," *Letter Book A.*

66. *Journal,* Kentucky House of Representatives (August 2, 1813), p. 17.

67. Shelby, "Isaac Shelby to Militiamen of Kentucky, July 31, 1813," *Letter Book A; Journal,* Kentucky House of Representatives (November 19, 1813), p. 21.

68. Meyer, *op. cit.,* p. 135; Richardson, *Messages* (December 7, 1813), I, 535.

69. Benjamin Cassedy, *History of Louisville* (Louisville, 1852), pp. 118-22.

70. The General Assembly took more specific notice of Isaac Shelby's activities. This body resolved, "That they cannot close their session without expressing the high estimation in which they hold the late conduct of their venerable chief magistrate, ISAAC SHELBY, in leading the Kentucky Militia into Upper Canada, to victory and to glory. The plans and execution of them, were not depictions of patriotism, with which others amuse the admiring multitude; they were splendid realities, which exact our gratitude and that of his country, and justly entitle him to the applause of posterity." *Acts,* Kentucky General Assembly (February 1, 1814), p. 228.

71. Darnell, *op. cit.;* Atherton, *op. cit.;* Northcutt, *Diary; Register,* ed. and pub. Glenn Clift, Kentucky Historical Society, LVI (April, 1958), 165-80; (July, 1958), 253-69; (October, 1958), 325-43; Quisenberry, "The Memoirs of Colonel Micah Taul," *op. cit.,* pp. 201-22.

72. "Tarrance Kirby to Abraham Lincoln, 1862." Original owned by William H. Townsend, Lexington, Kentucky.

73. This number is an approximation, as no one can know exactly how many were killed. Some sources say there were more than one hundred casualties. Glenn Clift, *Remember the Raisin!* (Frankfort, 1961), pp. 101-06.

74. *Military History of Kentucky,* pp. 98-118.

75. Clift, *Raisin!,* pp. 26-45; Darnell, *op. cit.,* pp. 37-41.

76. "Richard M. Johnson to Prospective Volunteers, March 23, 1813," *Military History of Kentucky,* pp. 86-88; Quisenberry, "The Memoirs of Colonel Micah Taul," *op. cit.,* pp. 201-08.

77. *Ibid.*

78. An interesting comment on this deficiency of supplies appears in: Shelby, "Isaac Shelby to William Eustis, August 28, 1812," *Letter Book A.*

79. *Acts,* Kentucky General Assembly, 1809-15.

INDEX

Adair, John, 93
Adams, Henry, causes of war of 1812, 9
Adams, John Q., letter to William Eustis, 13, 16 n. 8
Adams, Nathaniel, letter to brother cited, 16 n. 7
Allan, Ebenezer, and "The Canadian Volunteers," 46 n. 10
Allen, Colonel John, 88
 letter of cited, 89, 98 n. 57
American Revolution, aftermath, 3
Amherstburg, Upper Canada, 20, 34
 as British post, 63
 as Indian center, 4, 21, 63, 66
 garrisons for fort at, 39
 influence of British fur traders at, 63
 naval base at, 50
 reinforced by British, 33
Askin, Charles, behavior of Canadian militia at Battle of York, 38, 47 n. 35
Askin, John, Jr., leader of Ottawa raiding party, 64

Baby, Lieutenant-Colonel Baptiste, 33
Barclay, Robert H.
 at Amherstburg, 52, 54
 relinquished blockade of Erie, Pennsylvania, 55
Bay of Quinte, Upper Canada, militia from, 32
Beaver Dams, Upper Canada, outpost at, 42
Black Rock, New York, 34-35, 74
 naval base at, 51
Blount, Governor William, 90
Blythe, Reverend James, 85-86
Bostwick, Lieutenant-Colonel Henry
 as leader of attack on American raiders, 40
 defeated at Malcolm's Mills, 44
Bostwick, John, 40
Brant, Joseph, 63
British
 blamed for inciting Indians, 3
 policy toward Indians, 3
British Indian Department
 at Detroit, 68
 blamed for lack of Indian assistance, 69

Brock, Major-General Sir Isaac
 army career of, described, 18-19
 as military commander, 19
 assesses importance of Detroit victory, 24-25
 captures Detroit, 34
 captures Hull's records, 24
 death of, 26
 differences with Sir George Prevost, 25
 discussed probabilities of war with United States, 21
 effect of death of upon Canadian militia, 34
 evaluation of, 26-27
 importance of Detroit victory, 24
 letter to brother cited, 18
 letters to Prevost cited, 45, 48 n. 55, 54
 plans to capture Detroit, 23
 preparations for war, 17
 proposes new militia law, 31
 regard for Tecumseh, 20
 relations with Indians, 20
 succeeds Francis Gore as administrator of Upper Canada, 31
 training of militia, 31, 46 n. 9
Brock, Savery, 26
Brockville, Upper Canada, American attack upon, 36, 47 n. 29
Brown, James, letter of, cited, 79
Brownstown, Michigan Territory, skirmish at, 33
Buffalo, New York, 74
Burford Township, Upper Canada, 31
 defense of, 44
 militia from, 31
Burlington, Upper Canada, 39, 43
 fortifications at, 39
Butler, John, friendship with Indians, 61

Caldwell, James, letter to Senator Thomas Worthington cited, 16 n. 5
Campbell, Lieutenant-Colonel John
 conducted American raiding party, 43
 reprimanded, 43
Canada
 preparations for war, 4
 views on American agression, 5
Canadian Incorporated Militia, 44

99